love...
Sewing

love...
Sewing

25 SIMPLE STEP-BY-STEP
PROJECTS TO SEW

CHERYL OWEN

NEW HOLLAND

First published in 2011 by
New Holland Publishers (UK) Ltd
London • Cape Town • Sydney • Auckland

Garfield House
86-88 Edgware Road
London W2 2EA
United Kingdom
www.newhollandpublishers.com

80 McKenzie Street
Cape Town 8001
South Africa

Unit 1, 66 Gibbes Street
Chatswood, NSW 2067
Australia

218 Lake Road
Northcote, Auckland
New Zealand

10 9 8 7 6 5 4 3 2 1

ISBN 978 184773 592 8

Editor Clare Sayer
Photography Mark Winwood
Design Beverly Price, www.one2six.com
Production Laurence Poos
Editorial Direction Rosemary Wilkinson

Repro by Modern Age Repro House Ltd, Hong Kong
Printed and bound in Singapore by Tien Wah Press (PTE) Ltd

contents

introduction 6

the basics 8
   materials and equipment 10
   techniques 13

the projects 22
   cutwork cushion 24
   bolster cushion 28
   pyramid cushion 32
   box cushion 36
   tie-on cushion 40
   stationery folder 44
   ripple table runner 48
   bordered tablecloth 52
   bound napkin 56
   pocketed napkin 60
   place mat 64
   bordered throw 66
   patchwork play mat 68
   potpourri sachet 72
   clothes envelope 76
   tissue case 80
   drawstring bag 84
   shopping bag 88
   scallop cot quilt 92
   picnic rug 96
   beach bag 100
   wall tidy 104
   buttoned blind 108
   lampshade 112
   cupcake doorstop 116

templates 120
useful addresses 127
index 128

Introduction

The craft of sewing has been hugely popular for centuries, for both pleasure and practical purposes and with the fabulous choice of inexpensive fabrics that are widely available today, sewing has not lost its appeal. All the ideas in this book are not only beautiful to look at and fun to make but are useful too. Be inspired to make soft furnishings for the home and lifestyle accessories for yourself. Many of the projects would make lovely gifts for family and friends – if you can bear to part with them!

Those who love fabric will probably have a glorious stash of fabrics and trimmings waiting to be dipped into and turned into innovative creations. Large quantities of materials are not required so you may find inspiration for a favourite fabric you have been waiting to use. Most of the projects featured are quick to make so are ideal for a novice and those with little spare time. All the essential sewing techniques you need are explained in detail at the beginning of the book and each project has concise instructions and step-by-step photographs to guide you through.

Whether you are a complete beginner or are already a keen needleworker, you will soon be learning new skills or embarking on a new hobby such as patchwork or quilting. And, more importantly, you will have a collection of beautiful handmade items to add style and individuality to your home!

the basics

materials and equipment

Fabrics

Most of the projects in this book are made from cotton and linen, which are natural fibres that are easy to work with, so are ideal for beginners. Fabrics made from natural fibres are prone to shrink so it is advisable to wash fabrics before cutting out.

Cotton There is an enormous range of printed cotton fabrics available to buy online or from fabric and craft stores. Many are produced for patchwork and quilting purposes and are complemented by co-coordinating plain coloured cottons. Also consider cotton lace such as cutwork and broderie anglaise, which lend themselves to creating feminine gifts.

Linen This strong, natural fabric is available in different weights. Linen is expensive and creases easily but feels luxurious.

Furnishing fabric These durable fabrics are used to make soft furnishings. They come in lots of finishes and printed patterns and are usually 137 cm (54 in) wide.

Fleece and felt Fleece is also known as polar fleece. It has a combed nap which makes it warm and cosy. Iron fleece with a cool iron. Felt is a non-woven material, it is inexpensive and comes in a large range of colours. Fleece and felt don't fray so they are ideal to cut motifs from to add as decoration to your creations.

Interfacing Stiffen fabric with interfacing. Non-woven and woven varieties come in different weights to suit their purpose. They are sold in packs or by the metre. Press iron-on (fusible) interfacing or tack sew-in interfacing to the wrong side of the fabric.

Wadding Layer wadding between fabrics to pad them to make quilts. Cotton and eco-friendly bamboo wadding is available although polyester wadding is most commonly used. Wadding comes in different weights.

Tear-away stabilizer Place this non-woven material under fabric to be machine embroidered. It adds body and supports the fabric. Gently tear away the excess stabilizer after stitching.

Haberdashery

Most of the items mentioned here can be found in good department stores or specialist sewing shops. It's always a good idea to keep a collection of buttons, ribbons and other trimmings as you come across them – you will soon find a use for them!

Buttons Use buttons for decoration as well as practical purposes. There is a huge choice available. Flat buttons have flat backs with two or four holes. Shank buttons have a loop underneath to sew through. Self-cover buttons can be covered with your choice of fabric, they are simple to use and come in different sizes.

Ribbons Colourful ribbons come in all sorts of widths and finishes. They can be used purely for decoration, for loops, bag drawstrings and to create woven ribbon designs.

Zippers Use a zipper to close two edges of fabric temporarily such as on a cushion cover or a bag. Stitch the zipper in place with a zipper foot on a sewing machine.

Trimmings There is an exciting selection of trimmings available to finish your makes. Sew-on trimmings such as braid, piping, bead edging and bobble trim can neaten straight edges. Stitch braid on top close to both long edges, insert trimmings with a flat flange in a seam using a piping or zipper foot. Just a few beads hand sewn at random are a lovely finishing touch.

Threads Choose sewing thread to match the fabric colour, it should be strong and durable, with some 'give' in it. General-purpose mercerized cotton thread is suitable for woven natural fibre fabrics. General-purpose polyester thread is good on woven synthetic and knitted fabrics. Use the sewing thread or a heavy polyester thread for topstitching and sewing buttons. Generally, for patchwork and quilting use a 50 mercerized cotton thread. For professional results, use a machine embroidery thread for decorative zigzag stitching. Use embroidery threads such as widely available stranded cotton for hand embroidery and decorative running stitch. The skeins are made up of six strands which have to be separated for fine work.

D-rings D-rings are metal 'D' shaped rings used to secure straps and fastenings. They come in various sizes.

Bias binding This is a strip of bias-cut fabric with the edged pressed under for binding curved and straight edges. Buy bias binding by the metre (yard) or in packs. It comes in different widths, a range of colours and a limited range of patterns. Make your own with a bias binding maker.

Piping cord Cover this inexpensive cord with bias strips of fabric to make your own piping. It comes in different thicknesses.

Touch-and-close tape This is a two-part tape, one tape has a looped mesh surface and the other a hooked surface. The two layers interlock when pressed together. The tapes are available for sewing on or have a self-adhesive backing for sticking. Use touch-and-close tape to fix blinds to battens or to fasten bags. They are also available as discs.

Metal eyelets Metal eyelets are available in a few different sizes and have a nickel, gilt or painted finish.

Most come in a kit with a fixing tool, small eyelets can be fixed with special pliers.

Press studs Fasten bags or cushion covers with two-part metal or transparent plastic press studs.

Bag handles Bag handles can be made of various materials such as plastic, wood, metal and bamboo. Choose a style to suit the design and size of your bag. Using ready-made handles is a simple way to give a professional finish to the bag.

Equipment

Even if you are new to sewing, you will probably have some of the basic equipment needed to get started. Keep the tools together and use them only on fabric and their trimmings, otherwise they may become blunt and dirty. Work on a clean, well lit surface. Keep sharp tools beyond the reach of small children and pets.

Pattern-making papers Haberdashery stores supply pattern-making paper. Durable paper such as parcel paper is also suitable as it comes in large sizes. Tracing paper is useful for making patterns you will need to see through, for positioning motifs for example.

Pattern-making tools Use a fine pen or propelling pencil for accurate drawing. Draw straight lines against a ruler and describe circles with a pair of compasses. Use a set square to make accurate angles when drawing on paper and fabric.

Measuring tools A plastic-coated or cloth tape measure is useful for measuring curves. Use a metre (yard) stick to draw against for long lengths and to measure fabric quantities. A transparent 30 cm (12 in) ruler is a handy size for drawing patterns on paper and fabric and for checking measurements. A 15 cm (6 in) long sewing gauge has a slider to set at different levels for marking hems, seams and as a quilting guide.

Fabric-marking tools Draw on fabric with an air-erasable pen, the marks made will gradually fade away. Alternatively, use a water-soluble pen: the marks can be removed with water. Tailor's chalk comes in different colours, in wedge and pencil form. Marks will brush off although a slight mark may remain. Test all methods of marking fabric on scrap fabric first.

Scissors Cut paper patterns with paper scissors. Bent-handled dressmaking shears are comfortable and accurate to use for cutting fabric as the angle of the lower blade allows the fabric to lie flat. The shears are available in different lengths, so test before buying. A top-quality pair of shears is expensive but will last a lifetime. A small pair of sharp embroidery scissors is vital for snipping threads and seam allowances. Pinking shears cut a zigzag fray-resistant edge for neatening seams and to cut fabrics that are prone to fraying.

Needles Needles for sewing machines come in different sizes with different shaped points. The lower the number, the finer the point. Sizes 70–90 (9–14) are the most commonly used. A sharp-point needle is the most versatile for woven fabrics. Stitch non-woven fabrics with a ballpoint needle. In hand sewing needles, the higher the number the shorter and finer the needle. Use crewel embroidery needles for embroidery, they have a large eye so are easy to thread. Mattress needles are very long and are ideal for sewing through cushions, to attach buttons for example.

Pins Dressmaking pins come in various thicknesses, household pins are the most versatile. Use lace or bridal pins on delicate fabrics as other pins may mark the surface. Coloured glass-headed pins show up well on a large expanse of fabric. Quilting pins are extra long to push through the layers of a quilt, they have colourful shapely ends so are easy to see. Curved basting pins are curved safety pins. They are used to secure fabric layers together, be careful that they do not leave noticeable holes in the fabric.

Bodkin This needle-like tool has a large eye and blunt tip. Fasten a bodkin to a drawstring to draw it through a channel or to the end of a fabric tube to turn it right side out.

Rouleau turner Also known as a tube turner, a rouleau turner can be used in place of a bodkin. A latch hook at one end is hooked onto the end of a drawstring or fabric to draw it through the enclosure.

Bias binding maker Thread a bias or straight strip of fabric through this neat gadget, it will turn under the edges which you then press with an iron to make a binding. The bias binding maker comes in a range of widths.

techniques

The same basic methods occur throughout this book so read this section before embarking on any project and try out the techniques on scrap fabric before making the item. When following instructions, it is important to use metric or imperial measurements but not a combination of both.

Keep a basic sewing workbox to hand for all the projects. This should include dressmaking shears, embroidery scissors, ruler, tape measure, dressmaker's pins, a selection of sewing threads, a bodkin, an air-erasable pen or water-soluble pen or tailor's chalk.

Cutting out

Most of the projects in this book are made from squares and rectangles and can be drawn directly onto the fabric using a ruler and an air-erasable pen or water-soluble pen or tailor's chalk. There are also useful patterns and diagrams on page 120–126.

Woven fabrics stretch differently if pulled in different directions. The grain is the direction the threads are woven. The lengthwise grain is called the warp and runs parallel with the selvedges. The warp has less stretch which makes it easier to sew in this direction without the fabric stretching or puckering. The grain that runs across the fabric from selvedge to selvedge is the weft. It has a little more stretch than the warp. Cut rectangles and squares parallel with the warp and weft.

Most fabrics, especially printed ones, have a right and wrong side and in most cases it will be obvious which is the right side. Some fabrics, particularly plain woven ones, do not have a wrong side and are known as double-faced fabrics.

Using templates and patterns

Sewing patterns have an arrow on them which is the grain line. Keep the grain line parallel with the fabric selvedge when positioning the pattern. Lay the fabric smoothly out flat on a table or the floor to cut it out. To cut pairs of patterns, fold the fabric lengthwise or widthwise to make a double layer. Pin the pattern or draw it on top. If the pattern has a fold line, match the fold line to the folded edge of the fabric. Pin the layers together and cut them out. Otherwise, keep the fabric single. Mark the position of any dots on the fabric with a pin, an air-erasable pen or a water-soluble pen.

Positioning motifs

If your fabric has a distinctive motif, you may wish to show it whole, on the centre of a cushion for example. Make a pattern from tracing or greaseproof paper so you can see through it. Fold the pattern into quarters to find the centre then open it out flat again. Mark the seam allowance and grain line. Lay the pattern over the motif on the fabric, matching grain lines and the centre of the pattern to the centre of the design. Pin in place and cut out. You may need to buy a larger amount of fabric to allow for positioning motifs.

If the fabric has a repeat pattern, wide stripes or checks, centre these too so they will be positioned symmetrically when the item is made.

Stitching

Most of the projects in this book are worked using simple stitches on a sewing machine. Occasionally you will need to stitch by hand, when closing openings or tacking.

Tacking

Tacking are stitches that join fabric layers temporarily together. The more you stitch and gain confidence, the less reliant on tacking before stitching you will become. Tack by hand or use a long machine stitch. Tacking is always useful for tricky areas such as joining many layers of fabric, stitching corners or tight curves. Work tacking stitches in a contrast coloured thread so they are easy to see. Remove tacking stitches once the seam has been completed.

Seams

Before stitching, match the seam allowances and pin together. Position pins at right angles to the seam line which means you can stitch over them or insert the pins along the seam line and remove them as you stitch. Experiment and see which method you prefer, it could be a combination of both.

A flat seam is the most commonly used seam and occurs throughout these projects. With the right sides facing and raw edges of the seam allowance level, stitch the seam, keeping the same distance from the raw edges. Sewing machines have lines on the base plate that are standard seam allowance distances from the needle, keep the fabric raw edges level with the relevant line to keep the size of the seam allowance constant. Stitch back and forth to start and finish to stop the ends of the seam from unravelling.

Joining a curved edge to a straight edge is a little more difficult. To help the curve lay flat, snip into the curved seam allowance at regular intervals then pin and stitch the seam (see right, above).

To topstitch on the right side, stitch parallel with a seam to emphasize it and to hold the seam allowance in place. Use contrast coloured or thick topstitching thread to accentuate the stitching.

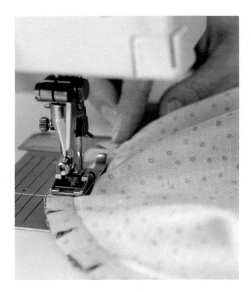

Layering seams

Reduce the bulk of fabric in the seam allowance by trimming the fabric in the seam allowance by different amounts after the seam has been stitched (see right, below).

Neatening seams

Protect raw edges that will be prone to wear with a zigzag stitch.

Set the stitch width to about 3 mm (⅛ in) wide and 3 mm (⅛ in) apart then stitch along the raw edges. Alternatively, trim the seam with a pair of pinking shears.

Clipping corners and curves

Use embroidery scissors to carefully snip 'V' shapes into curved seam allowances and across corners. This will help the fabric lay flat when it is turned through to the right side. Take care not to snip the stitching.

Slipstitching

Slipstitching is used to join two folded edges or one folded edge to a flat surface such as closing a gap in a seam or to secure binding.

Keep the stitches small. Working from right to left with a single thread, bring the needle out through one folded edge. Pick up a few threads on the opposite edge and insert the needle back through the folded edge about 6 mm (¼ in) along from where it emerged. Repeat along the length.

Using bias strips

Strips cut on the bias can be used to make bias binding, piping and rouleaux. The bias is any direction on the fabric that is not the warp or weft. The bias will stretch so take care when stitching along the bias as seams will stretch.

Cutting bias strips

Press the fabric diagonally at a 45-degree angle to the selvedge. This diagonal fold is the true bias. Press along the fold then open out flat. With an air-erasable pen, water-soluble pen or tailor's chalk and ruler, draw lines the width of the bias strip parallel with the pressed line. To make bindings and piping, add 10 cm (4 in) to the desired length for easing and turning under the ends. Add extra for joins.

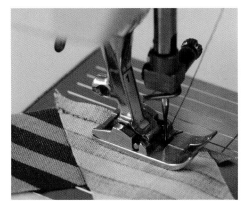

Joining bias strips

Position one end of two strips at right angles with the right sides facing and matching the raw ends. Stitch the bias strips together taking 6 mm (¼ in) seam allowance. Press the seam open and cut off the extending corners.

Bindings

Although ready-made bias binding is widely available, it is economical and quick to make your own. Curved edges must be bound with bias binding; straight edges can be bound with bias or straight binding.

Create single bias or straight binding with a bias binding maker. The manufacturer's instructions will indicate the width to cut the binding.

Making bias binding

Push the strip (wrong side up) through the wide end of a bias binding maker. If necessary, poke a pin through the gap in the top of the bias binding maker to ease the binding through. The edges will be turned under as the binding emerges out of the narrow end, press in place as you pull the binding through.

Attaching single binding

1 Open out one folded edge of the binding. With right sides facing and matching the raw edges, pin the binding to the fabric. Stitch along the fold line.

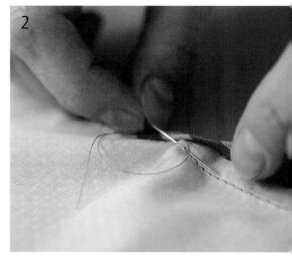

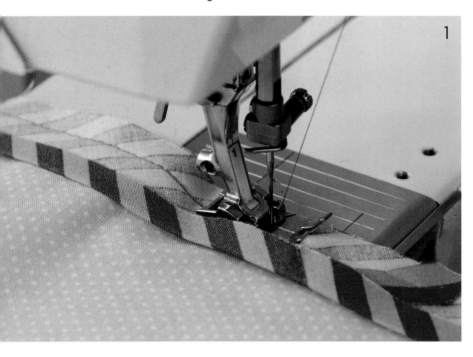

2 Turn the binding to the underside, matching the pressed edge to the seam. Pin then slipstitch the pressed edge along the seam.

Attaching double binding

Make double binding from bias or straight strips. Press the strips lengthwise in half with wrong sides facing. Pin and stitch the binding to the fabric, matching the raw edges. Turn the binding to the underside. Pin then slipstitch the pressed edge along the seam or topstitch in place.

Piping

Piping gives a professional finish to cushions and other items. Ready-made piping comes in a limited range of colours and is costly so make your own using inexpensive piping cord.

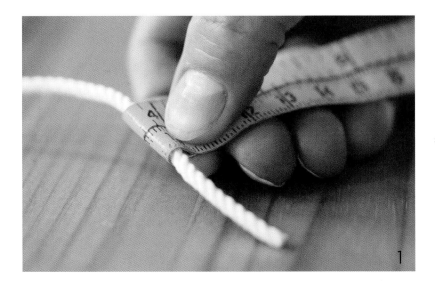

Making piping

1 Measure the circumference of the piping cord and add 3 cm (1 ¼ in) for the seam allowances. Cut a bias strip of fabric in this width that is the length required plus 10 cm (4 in) for ease and joining. Join bias strips if necessary.

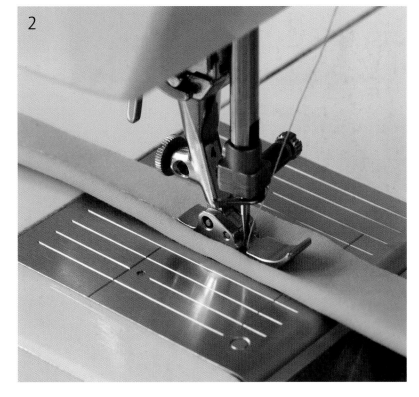

2 Lay the cord along the centre of the strip on the wrong side. Set the sewing machine to a long straight stitch length for machine tacking. Fold the strip lengthwise in half, enclosing the cord. Using a piping or zipper foot, stitch close to the piping cord.

Joining piping ends

1 To join the ends of piping neatly, allow a 2.5 cm (1 in) overlap. Pin the piping in place to 5 cm (2 in) each side of the overlap. Unpick the piping tacking for 5 cm (2 in) each side of the overlap to reveal the cord. Cut off 2.5 cm (1 in) on half the strands at each end of the cord to thin it.

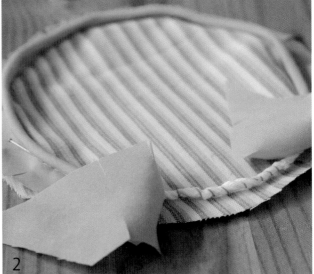

2 Twist the ends of the cord together and bind with thread, make a few stitches to hold the cord together.

3 Wrap one end of the piping strip around the cord again. Turn under 6 mm (¼ in) on the other end and wrap it around the cord. Tack the cord in place ready for stitching.

Attaching piping

If the piping is to be stitched to a curved edge, snip the seam allowance at regular intervals so the seam allowance lays flat when applied to the curve. Pin the piping to the right side of the fabric, matching the raw edges. Snip the seam allowance at any corners. Tack in place by hand or machine using a piping or zipper foot.

Rouleaux

A rouleau is a fine tube of bias cut fabric. It has many uses such as loops for fastening buttons, ties for fastening or purely for decoration. Being bias cut, the rouleau bends easily, see the lampshade on page 112.

1 Cut a bias strip of fabric. When calculating the size, double the required width and allow two 6-7.5 mm (¼-⁵⁄₁₆ in) seam allowances. Add extra to the length for turning in ends or inserting in seams. Join bias strips if necessary. Fold lengthwise in half with right sides facing. Stitch the long raw edges.

2 To turn right side out, fasten a bodkin to one end of the tube with a short length of thread. Ease the bodkin through the tube and it will pull the rouleau right side out. Alternatively, slip a rouleau turner into the tube, hook the end onto the end of the tube and pull through. If the rouleau has wrinkled, steam it with a steam iron held just above the wrinkles.

the projects

cutwork cushion

This beautiful cushion is surprisingly simple to make. A layer of coloured cutwork lace is applied over a contrast coloured fabric which shows through the cutwork shapes. If you cannot find a coloured cutwork lace, dye white cutwork cotton lace to achieve the effect.

you will need

- 40 cm (16 in) square of pink cutwork cotton lace fabric

- 40 cm (½ yd) of 112 cm (44 in) wide pale green plain cotton fabric

- matching sewing threads

- 4 x 2-cm (¾-in) diameter buttons

- 35 cm (13¾ in) square cushion pad

1 For the cushion front, cut a 38 cm (15 in) square of cutwork lace and plain fabric. Pin the cutwork lace on top of the plain fabric with right sides facing up. Tack the outer edges together.

2 For the cushion backs, cut out two 38 x 27.5 cm (15 x 10¾ in) rectangles of plain fabric. Press under 1.5 cm (⅝ in) then 4.5 cm (1¾ in) on one long edge of each back. Stitch close to the inner pressed edge to form a button stand. Using your sewing machine, stitch four buttonholes, equally spaced along one button stand. Cut the buttonholes open.

3 With right sides facing up, overlap the back cushion that has the buttonholes over the button stand on the other back cushion by 5 cm (2 in). Tack across the ends of the button stands.

4 Mark the button positions at the centre of the buttonholes with pins. Sew a button at each pin position on the underlying button stand.

5 With right sides facing, pin the front and back cushions together. Stitch the outer edges taking 1.5 cm (⅝ in) seam allowance. Clip the corners and turn the cushion right side out. Insert the cushion pad and fasten the buttons.

bolster cushion

Here is a classic bolster cushion brought up to date with a contemporary patterned cover with contrast ends. Piping gives the cushion an elegant finish but can be omitted if you prefer.

you will need

- 60 cm (⅔ yd) of 112 cm (44 in) wide blue with green patterned cotton fabric

- 30 cm (⅓ yd) of 112 cm (44 in) wide lime green with turquoise patterned cotton fabric

- matching sewing threads

- 40 cm (16 in) zipper

- 120 cm (1⅓ yd) of 3 mm (⅛ in) diameter piping cord

- 45 x 17 cm (18 x 6⅝ in) bolster cushion pad

1 Cut a 56 x 48 cm (22⅛ x 19 in) rectangle of pale blue with green patterned fabric. With right sides facing, fold the rectangle in half parallel with the short edges. Tack the short edges together taking 1.5 cm (⅝ in) seam allowance, forming a tube. Stitch for 4 cm (1⅝ in) at each end of the tacked seam. Do not remove the tacking. Press the seam open.

3 Using a zipper foot on the sewing machine, stitch the zip in place 6 mm (¼ in) from the tacked seam and across the ends of the zip. Take care not to sew through to the underside of the tube. Remove the tacking and open the zip.

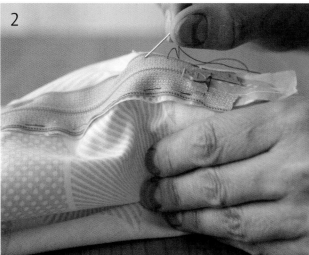

2 Place the zip centrally along the seam, face down. Pin and tack the zip in position, put your hand inside the tube to support the fabric and to help avoid sewing through to the underside of the tube. Turn the tube right side out.

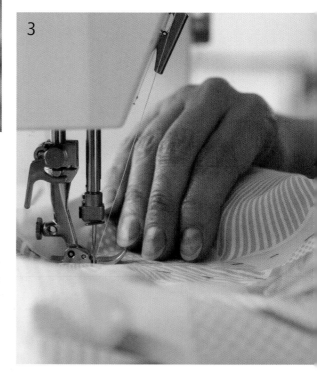

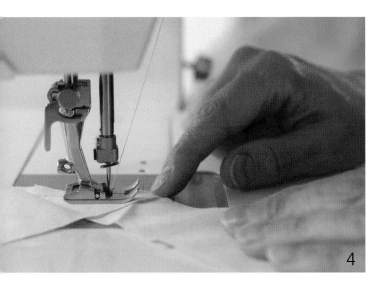

4 Cut two 20 cm (8 in) diameter circles of lime green with turquoise patterned fabric. Cut 4 cm (1⅝ in) wide bias strips measuring a total of 120 cm (47¼ in) in length for the piping. Join the strips to make a continuous length, referring to the Joining Bias Strips technique on page 17.

5 Refer to pages 19–20 to make and attach piping to the circumference of the circles taking 1.5 cm (⅝ in) seam allowance, snip the seam allowance of the piping so it lays flat on the curves of the circles. Join the piping ends to make a neat ring of piping.

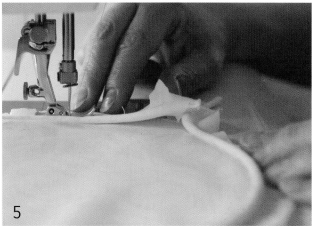

6 Fold the circles and ends of the tube into quarters, mark the edges of the fabric with a pin at each quarter mark. Snip the seam allowance of the tube at 1 cm (⅜ in) intervals, this will help the seam allowance to lay flat. With right sides facing, pin the circles to each end of the tube, matching the quarter marks.

7 Using a zipper or piping foot on the sewing machine, tack and stitch the circles to the tube, taking 1.5 cm (⅝ in) seam allowance. Trim the seam allowances to layer them. Snip the curves and turn right side out. Insert the cushion pad and close the zip.

pyramid cushion

The unusual shape of this funky cushion is created with a few cleverly positioned seams which are highlighted with a colourful bobble trim. Make the cushion from striped fabric to emphasize the shape.

you will need

- 50 cm (½ yd) of 90 cm (36 in) wide green and yellow striped cotton fabric
- matching sewing threads
- 80 cm (1 yd) of yellow bobble trim
- 400 g (14 oz) of polyester toy filling

1 Cut a rectangle of striped fabric 83 x 43 cm (32¾ x 17 in). Cut two 40 cm (15¾ in) lengths of bobble trim. Pin and tack one length of bobble trim to one long edge of the rectangle between the centre and 1.5 cm (⅝ in) in from one short edge on the right side, allowing a 1.5 cm (⅝ in) seam allowance.

2 With right sides facing, fold the rectangle in half parallel with the short edges. Pin the short and side tacked edges together. Using a zipper or piping foot, stitch in place, taking 1.5 cm (⅝ in) seam allowance, leaving an 18 cm (7 in) gap to turn through. Clip the corners then press the seam open.

3 Mark the centre of the remaining bobble trim with a pin. Open out the raw edges of the cushion. Tack the trim to the raw edge on the right side, matching the pin to the seam, allowing a 1.5 cm (⅝ in) seam allowance.

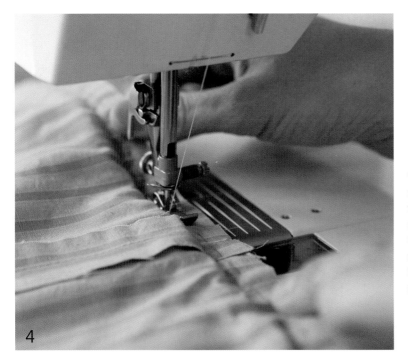

4 Fold the cushion at each end of the tacked bobble trim, with right sides facing. Adjust the seam to lie across the centre of the cushion, pin the raw edges together. Using a piping or zipper foot to accommodate the bobble trim, stitch in place, taking 1.5 cm (⅝ in) seam allowance. Clip the corners.

5 Turn the cushion right side out and fill firmly with the toy filling. Slipstitch the opening edges closed.

box cushion

This chunky cushion is a comfortable addition to the house or garden. The softly padded edges are hand stitched and the centre is buttoned with self-cover buttons to match the contrast coloured sides of the cushion. The cushion is 40 cm (16 in) square and has a practical carrying handle.

you will need

- 30 cm (⅓ yd) of 112 cm (44 in) wide green dotted cotton fabric

- 10 cm (¼ yd) of 90 cm (36 in) wide lightweight sew-in interfacing

- 50 cm (½ yd) of 112 cm (44 in) wide pink with green spotted cotton fabric

- matching sewing threads, pink embroidery thread, button thread

- 400 g (14 oz) toy filling

- quilting pins

- large crewel needle

- mattress needle

- 8 x 3 cm (1¼ in) self-cover buttons

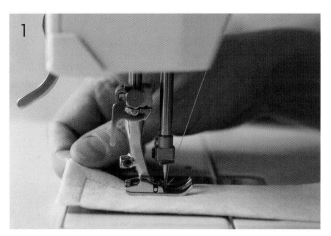

1

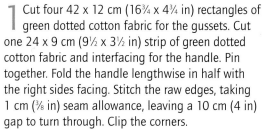

1 Cut four 42 x 12 cm (16¾ x 4¾ in) rectangles of green dotted cotton fabric for the gussets. Cut one 24 x 9 cm (9½ x 3½ in) strip of green dotted cotton fabric and interfacing for the handle. Pin together. Fold the handle lengthwise in half with the right sides facing. Stitch the raw edges, taking 1 cm (⅜ in) seam allowance, leaving a 10 cm (4 in) gap to turn through. Clip the corners.

2 Trim the seam allowance to layer it (see layering seams technique, page 15). Turn the handle right side out and press. Slipstitch the opening closed. Pin the handle centrally to the right side of one gusset. Stitch a 2.5 cm (1 in) square at each end of the handle, stitch a cross shape across the square.

2

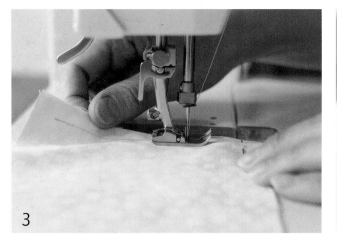

3

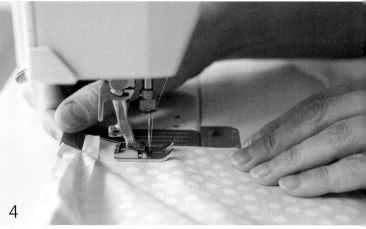

4

3 With right sides facing and taking 1 cm (⅜ in) seam allowance, pin and stitch two gussets together along the short edges, starting and finishing the stitching 1 cm (⅜ in) from the long edges. Repeat to join all the gussets. Cut two 42 cm (16¾ in) squares of pink with green spotted cotton fabric for the top and base.

4 With right sides facing and matching the gusset seams to the corners of the top cushion, pin and stitch the upper edges of the gussets to the cushion, pivoting the seams at the corners. Snip the corners and press the seams open. Repeat to stitch the base to the lower edges of the gussets, leaving 25 cm (10 in) to turn through.

5 Turn the cushion right side out and fill firmly and evenly with toy filling. Slipstitch the opening closed. Fold the top of the cushion along one seam and pin the top and gusset together 2 cm (¾ in) from the seam using quilting pins.

6 Thread a large crewel needle with a double length of embroidery thread. Knot the thread ends. Starting 2 cm (¾ in) in from one corner, sew through both layers with a running stitch 2 cm (¾ in) from the seams around the top of the cushion. Repeat on the base of the cushion.

7 Cover eight 3 cm (1¼ in) self-cover buttons with green dotted fabric following the button manufacturer's instructions. Mark four button positions on the top and base of the cushion with pins 12.5 cm (5 in) in from the side edges. Thread a mattress needle with a double length of button thread. Tie the thread ends to the shank of the button. Insert the needle through the cushion at the first button position and bring it out under the cushion at the corresponding position.

8 Cut off the needle. Thread one end of the thread through the shank of a button and tie it to the other thread, pulling the threads to dimple the cushion. Tie the threads securely together. Cut the thread ends under the button. Repeat to attach the other buttons.

tie-on cushion

Make relaxing in a sunny garden especially pleasant with a custom-made cushion to sit on. This cushion has ties at the back to fasten around the back struts of a chair. The cushion filling is anchored in place using a traditional tufting upholstery technique.

you will need

- pattern paper or parcel paper
- 4 cm (1½ in) diameter button
- approximately 60 cm (⅔ yd) of 112 cm (44 in) wide pink striped cotton fabric
- matching sewing threads
- approximately 150 g (5 oz) polyester toy filling
- 1.8 cm (¾ in) bias binding maker
- 1 skein of pink stranded cotton embroidery thread
- mattress needle
- button thread
- 4 x 1.2 cm (½ in) diameter buttons

1 To make a pattern, draw a rectangle or square that is the size of the seat on pattern or parcel paper. Add 2.5 cm (1 in) to the front and side edges. Draw around a 4 cm (1½ in) diameter button to round the corners. Add a 7.5 mm (⁵⁄₁₆ in) seam allowance on all edges. Cut out the pattern. Use the pattern to cut two cushions from fabric.

2 Cut four 40 x 3.5 cm (16 x 1⅜ in) bias strips of fabric for the ties. With right sides facing, fold and pin the ties lengthwise. Stitch the long edges, taking 6 mm (¼ in) seam allowance. Use a bodkin to turn the ties right side out. Turn in one end of each tie and slipstitch the ends closed.

3 Pin and tack the raw ends of the ties to the back edge of one cushion on the right side 3.5 cm (1⅜ in) then 8.5cm (3⅜ in) in from the side edges. With wrong sides facing, pin the cushions together.

4 Cut 3.5 cm (1⅜ in) wide bias strips measuring the circumference of the cushion plus 10 cm (4 in) in length for the binding. Join the strips if necessary and make a continuous length of bias binding using a 1.8 cm (¾ in) bias binding maker, referring to the Joining Bias Strips and Making Bias Binding techniques on page 17.

5 Press under one end of the binding to start. Pin the binding to the cushion, taking 7.5 mm ($^5/_{16}$ in) seam allowance. Stitch, leaving a 15 cm (6 in) gap at the back. Ease the binding around the corners. Cut off the excess binding 1.5 cm ($^5/_8$ in) beyond the start of the binding.

6 Stuff the cushion firmly. Pin, tack and stitch the gap closed, taking 7.5 mm ($^5/_{16}$ in) seam allowance. Fold the binding over the edge of the cushion and slipstitch the pressed edge along the seam.

7 Cut embroidery thread into four 25 cm (10 in) lengths. Cut the remaining thread into 4.5 cm (1$^3/_4$ in) lengths. Divide into four bunches and tie each bunch tightly around the centre with a 25 cm (10 in) length to make a tuft. Fold the tuft at the centre, trim the thread ends level and cut the ties to the same length.

8 Mark four tuft positions on top of the cushion with pins. Thread a mattress needle with a double length of button thread. Insert the needle up through the underside of the cushion and out through the top at the first tuft position. Loop the thread around the centre of one tuft and insert the needle back through the cushion.

9 Insert the needle through the hole of a button, insert the ends of the threads through the other buttonhole. Pull the threads tight to dimple the cushion, tie the thread ends securely together on top of the button. Cut off the excess thread. Repeat to attach the other buttons.

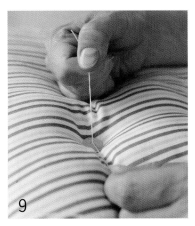

stationery folder

Keep A5 size paper and envelopes or postcards in this smart stationery folder. As a finishing touch, choose a beautiful button to use as a feature for the loop fastening. The folder would also make a delightful place to store treasured letters.

you will need

- 30 cm (⅓ yd) of 112 cm (44 in) wide blue dotted cotton fabric

- 30 cm (⅓ yd) of 112 cm (44 in) wide pink patterned cotton fabric

- matching sewing threads

- 30 cm (⅓ yd) of 90 cm (36 in) wide stiff iron-on interfacing

- 3 cm (1¼ in) diameter turquoise button

1 Use the template on page 120 to cut two pockets from blue dotted cotton fabric. Neaten the upper long edges of the pockets with a zigzag stitch. Press under 2 cm (¾ in) on the upper edges. Stitch close to the zigzagged edges to hem the pockets.

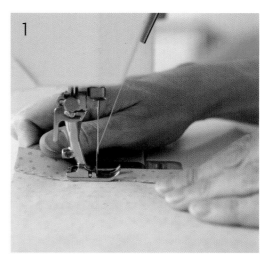

2 Cut two 27 x 19.5 cm (10⅝ x 7⅝ in) rectangles of both fabrics and interfacing. With right sides facing up, pin and tack the pockets to the lower section of the blue dotted rectangles which will be the linings, matching the raw edges. Fuse the interfacing to the wrong side of the pink patterned rectangles which will be the covers.

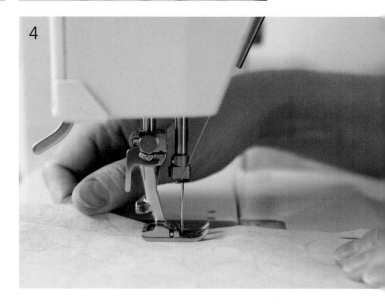

3 Cut an 11 x 3 cm (4⅜ x 1¼ in) bias strip of blue dotted fabric for the button loop. Fold in half lengthwise with right sides facing. Stitch the long edges taking 6 mm (¼ in) seam allowance. Turn right side out with a bodkin to make a button loop. Tack the ends of the loop centrally to the right hand long edge of one cover on the right side, this will·be the back.

4 With right sides facing, pin the covers on top of the linings. Taking 1.5 cm (⅝ in) seam allowance, stitch the raw edges, leaving the long left hand edge of the back cover and long right hand edge of the other cover open. Trim the seam allowance to layer it. Snip the corners. Turn right side out and press.

5 With the covers facing out and all edges level, pin the raw edges of the covers together. Cut a 27 x 10 cm (10⅝ x 3⅞ in) bias strip of blue dotted fabric. Press the strip lengthwise in half to make a double bias binding.

6 Matching the raw edges, pin and tack the binding to the front cover with 1.5 cm (⅝ in) extending at both ends. Stitch the binding to the folder taking 1.5 cm (⅝ in) seam allowance.

7 Pin under the ends of the binding. Fold the pressed edge of the binding to the back cover. Slipstitch along the seam. Sew a button to the front of the folder under the button loop.

ripple table runner

A table runner adds a touch of glamour to the dinner table. This colourful linen runner is shot through with sparkly metallic threads making it ideal for a party. The unusual ripple effect on the rows of tucks is easy to achieve. The runner measures 150 x 30 cm (60 x 12 in). Buying the quantity of fabric listed below will provide enough fabric to make a set of matching napkins too.

you will need

- 180 cm (2 yd) of 137 cm (54 in) wide metallic turquoise linen

- matching machine embroidery thread

1 Cut a 178 x 35 cm (68½ x 13¾ in) rectangle of fabric for the runner. With wrong sides facing, press under 17 cm (6¾ in) at one end of the runner. Stitch across the runner, 1 cm (⅜ in) from the pressed edge to form the first tuck.

2 To form the next tuck, fold and press across the runner 2 cm (¾ in) from the stitched line. Stitch across the runner, 1 cm (⅜ in) from the pressed edge to form the second tuck. Repeat to stitch and press a total of five tucks. Repeat at the other end of the runner.

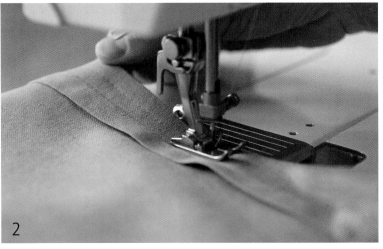

3 Press the tucks toward the centre of the runner. Tack across the ends of the tucks. Stitch at right angles across the tucks 8.5 cm (3⅜ in) in from and parallel with both long edges.

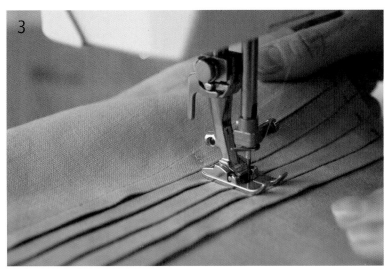

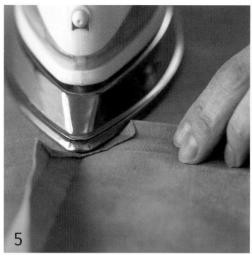

4 To hem the runner, press under 1 cm (⅜ in) then 1.5 cm (⅝ in) on the raw edges. Open out the fabric at the corners and cut diagonally across the allowance 6 mm (¼ in) from the pressed corner.

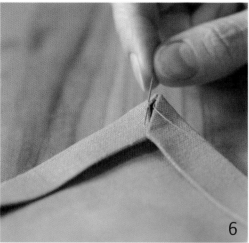

5 Press under the diagonal edge. Refold the hem – the diagonally folded edges should meet edge to edge.

6 Slipstitch the mitred edges together. Stitch close to the inner edges of the entire hem.

7 Press the centre of the tucks in the opposite direction towards the short edges of the runner.

bordered tablecloth

If you have never tried patchwork, this pretty tablecloth is an ideal project as the contrasting border is joined with the simplest patchwork technique. The tablecloth measures 150 cm (58 in) square.

you will need

- 140 cm (1¾ yd) of 112 cm (44 in) wide turquoise spotted cotton fabric

- 110 cm (1¼ in) of 112 cm (44 in) wide green floral cotton fabric

- matching sewing threads

1 Cut one 108 cm (42½ in) square and four 26.5 cm (10⅜ in) squares of turquoise spotted fabric. Cut four 108 x 26.5 cm (42½ x 10⅜ in) strips of green floral cotton fabric for the borders. With right sides facing, stitch a border strip to two opposite edges of the tablecloth taking 1.5 cm (⅝ in) seam allowance. Press the seams toward the borders. Neaten the seams with a zigzag stitch.

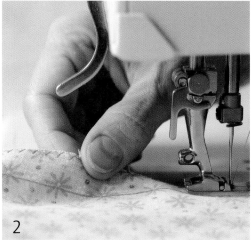

2 With right sides facing, stitch the small squares of tablecloth fabric to each end of the remaining border strips taking 1.5 cm (⅝ in) seam allowance. Press the seams toward the border then neaten the seams with a zigzag stitch.

3 With right sides facing, pin the border strips and small squares to the raw edges of the tablecloth, matching the seams. Insert a pin through the seams to match them. Stitch, taking a 1.5 cm (⅝ in) seam allowance. Press the seams toward the border. Neaten the seams with a zigzag stitch.

4 To hem the tablecloth, press under 1 cm (⅜ in) then 1.5 cm (⅝ in) on the raw edges. Open out the fabric at the corners and cut diagonally across the allowance 6 mm (¼ in) from the pressed corner.

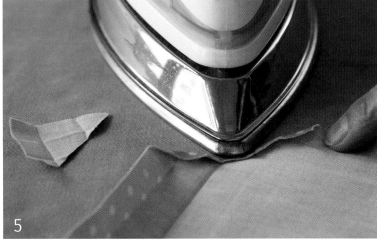

5 Press under the diagonal edge for 6 mm (¼ in). Refold the hem – the diagonally folded edges should meet edge to edge.

6 Slipstitch the mitred edges together. Stitch close to the inner edges of the entire hem.

bound napkin

Use this neat binding technique to finish the edges of napkins, tablecloths, runners and throws. Make a smart set of napkins to coordinate with a tablecloth or match the border to the colour scheme of your china.

you will need

- 20 cm (¼ yd) of 112 cm (44 in) wide turquoise spotted cotton fabric (for the binding)

- 40 cm (15¾ in) square of green floral cotton fabric (for the napkin)

- matching sewing threads

1 Cut two 82 cm (32¾ in) straight strips of 8 cm (3 in) wide turquoise spotted fabric for the binding. With right sides facing, join the lengths, taking 6 mm (¼ in) seam allowance to make a continuous length. Press the seam open. Press the binding lengthwise in half. Open out the binding and press the long edges to meet at the centre.

2 Open out the binding at one end and press under 6 mm (¼ in). With the right sides facing and starting halfway along one edge of the napkin, pin and stitch the binding to the napkin, taking a 2 cm (¾ in) seam allowance. Stitch along the fold line, finishing 2 cm (¾ in) from the adjacent edge.

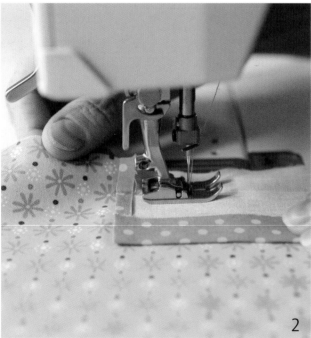

3 With wrong sides facing, fold the binding at a 45-degree angle from the corner. Next, fold the binding level with the stitched raw edges to lie along the adjacent edge of the napkin.

4 Mark the end of the previous stitching with a pin and stitch from this mark, finishing 2 cm (¾ in) from the next adjacent edge. Continue all the way around the napkin, overlapping the pressed end of the binding.

5 Press the binding outwards from the napkin then turn it to the underside along the centre fold line.

6 Pin the binding to the underside, folding under the fullness at the corners in a neat mitre. Slipstitch the pressed edges along the seams.

pocketed napkin

Make a set of pocketed napkins for a special occasion. The napkin edges are neatened with a wide zigzag stitch using a glossy machine embroidery thread. Trim the pocket with a pretty party decoration, a bead or a button and slip a small gift or greeting card inside.

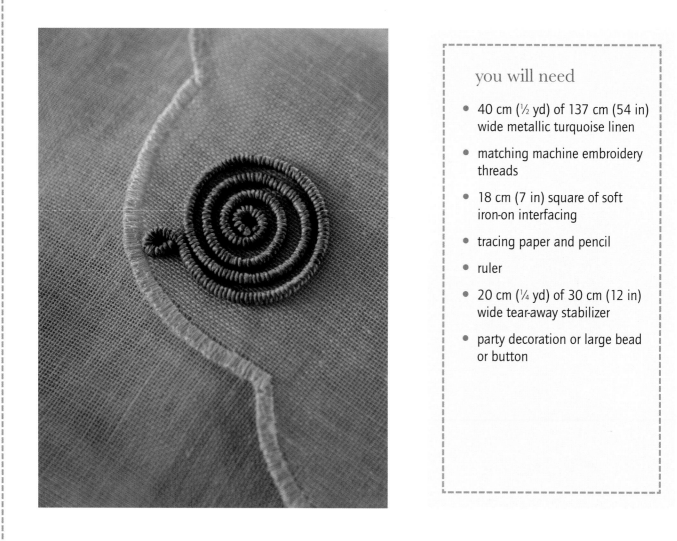

you will need

- 40 cm (½ yd) of 137 cm (54 in) wide metallic turquoise linen
- matching machine embroidery threads
- 18 cm (7 in) square of soft iron-on interfacing
- tracing paper and pencil
- ruler
- 20 cm (¼ yd) of 30 cm (12 in) wide tear-away stabilizer
- party decoration or large bead or button

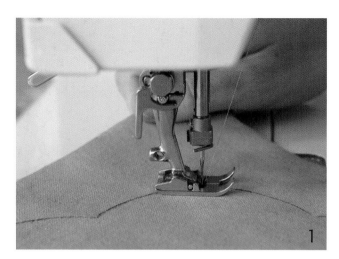

1 Cut an 18 cm (7 in) square of fabric. Fuse the interfacing to the fabric square. Use the template on page 121 to cut the pocket from tracing paper. Pin the template on the fabric matching the outer straight edges to two adjacent fabric edges. Draw around the curves with an air-erasable fabric pen. Use a straight stitch to stitch along the curved line with machine embroidery thread.

2 Set the sewing machine to a close zigzag stitch at the widest stitch width. Stitch along the curved line, with the straight stitching centred. To turn the stitching at the corners, keep the needle inserted at the inside edge of a corner, lift the presser foot and pivot the fabric. Continue stitching the pocket.

3 Carefully trim away the excess fabric outside the curved zigzag stitched line with a pair of sharp embroidery scissors. Draw the inner straight lines on the right side of the pocket with an air-erasable fabric pen and ruler.

4 Cut a 40 cm (16 in) square of fabric for the napkin. Using an air-erasable fabric pen and ruler, draw a 2.5 cm (1 in) margin inside the edges of the napkin. Pin the pocket to one corner of the napkin, matching the raw edges.

5 Cut four 40 x 4 cm (16 x 1½ in) strips of tear-away stabilizer. Pin a strip of the stabilizer under each edge of the napkin. Set the sewing machine to a straight stitch. On the right sides, stitch along the straight drawn lines.

6 Set the sewing machine to a close zigzag stitch at the widest stitch width. Stitch along the straight lines with the straight stitching centred. To turn the stitching at the corners, keep the needle inserted at the outside edge of a corner, lift the presser foot and pivot the fabric. Continue stitching the napkin edges. To finish, overlap the zigzag stitching by 1 cm (⅜ in).

7 Leave the trailing ends of thread. Pull the threads to the wrong side, thread them through a needle and work the threads through the back of the zigzag stitching for about 3 cm (1¼ in). Cut off the excess threads. Gently pull away the tear-away stabilizer on each side of the zigzag stitching.

8 Carefully trim away the excess fabric outside the zigzag stitching with a pair of sharp embroidery scissors. Sew a party decoration or large bead to the pocket.

TIP Test the zigzag stitching on a scrap of fabric with a piece of tear-away stabilizer underneath before embarking on the napkin.

place mat

This pretty place mat measures a generous 40 x 30 cm (15¾ x 12 in). A layer of curtain interlining inside provides added protection to the surface underneath and will slightly cushion the crockery.

you will need

- 40 cm (½ yd) of 137 cm (54 in) wide pale blue linen

- 40 cm (½ yd) of 112 cm (44 in) wide turquoise striped cotton fabric

- 70 cm of 1 cm (⅜ in) wide turquoise spotted ribbon

- matching sewing threads

- 40 cm (½ yd) of 137 cm (54 in) wide curtain interlining

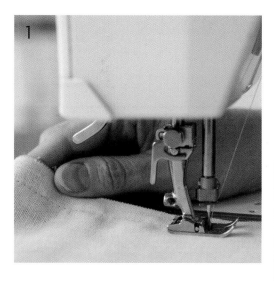

1 Cut a 33 x 27 cm (13¼ x 10¾ in) rectangle of pale blue linen and two 33 x 11 cm (13¼ x 4⅜ in) rectangles of turquoise striped fabric. With right sides facing, stitch the pale blue linen rectangle between the striped rectangles along the long edges, taking a 1.5 cm (⅝ in) seam allowance. Press the seams open.

2 Cut two 33 cm (13¼ in) lengths of spotted ribbon. On the right side, centre each length over a seam and pin in place. Stitch close to the edges of the ribbons.

3 Cut a 43 x 33 cm (17 x 13¼ in) rectangle of curtain interlining and pale blue linen. Lay the interlining out flat. Place the stitched place mat right side up on top, smooth the fabric outwards. Pin the pale blue rectangle on top with right sides facing.

4 Stitch the outer edges, taking 1.5 cm (⅝ in) seam allowance and leaving a 15 cm (6 in) gap to turn through. Clip the corners then carefully trim the interlining close to the seam. Turn the place mat right side out. Press the edges. Slipstitch the gap closed.

bordered throw

Transform an inexpensive chenille throw by adding a deep border of patterned fabric. The throw has neat mitred corners and measures approximately 170 x 135 cm (67 x 53 in). Alternatively, use a piece of chenille or woollen fabric to make the throw.

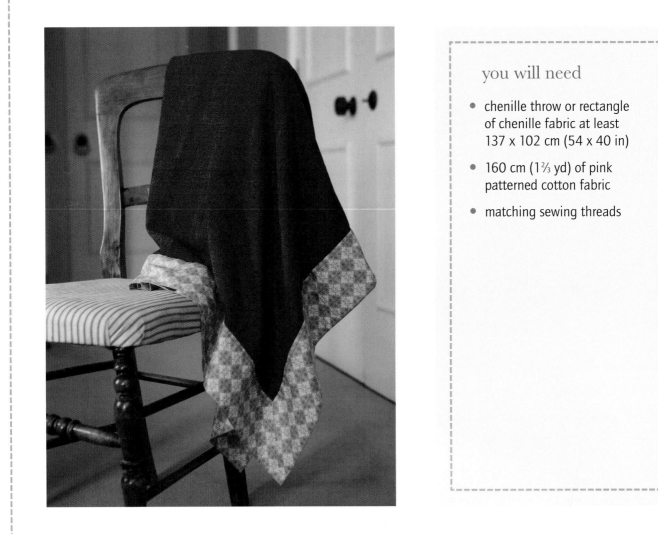

you will need

- chenille throw or rectangle of chenille fabric at least 137 x 102 cm (54 x 40 in)

- 160 cm (1⅔ yd) of pink patterned cotton fabric

- matching sewing threads

1

1 Cut a rectangle of chenille 133 x 98 cm (52⅜ x 38⅝ in). Cut two strips of pink patterned cotton fabric for the border 156 x 23 (61⁷⁄₁₆ x 9⅛ in). Refer to the diagram on page 122 to cut the ends of the borders to points. Press under 1.5 cm (⅝ in) on one long edge of each border.

2 With right sides facing and matching the pressed edges, stitch the short borders between the long borders at the mitred ends, finishing 1.5 cm (⅝ in) from the long raw edges. Clip the corners. Press the seams open, using a moistened finger to finger-press inside the corner where the iron will not reach.

2

3

4

3 With right sides facing, pin and stitch the long raw edges of the border to the throw taking 1.5 cm (⅝ in) seam allowance and pivoting the seam at the corners. Press the seam toward the border. Trim the seam allowance on the rectangle to 1 cm (⅜ in) to layer the seam.

4 Pin the pressed edges of the border along the seam. Press the border in half. Slipstitch the pressed edge along the seam.

patchwork play mat

Here is a fun project which would be a delightful gift for a young child. The softly padded play mat is made up of patchwork squares and is an ideal introductory patchwork project. The play mat measures 105 cm (41½ in) square and is spot quilted with felt starfish.

you will need

- 70 cm (¾ yd) of 112 cm (44 in) wide turquoise patterned cotton fabric

- 220 cm (2½ yd) of 112 cm (44 in) wide pink patterned cotton fabric

- matching sewing threads

- 110 cm (1¼ yd) of 114 cm (45 in) wide 113 g (4 oz) wadding

- curved basting pins (optional)

- 5 cm (2 in) bias binding maker

- 23 cm (9 in) square of yellow felt

- large-eyed needle

- shaded turquoise 3-ply cotton embroidery thread

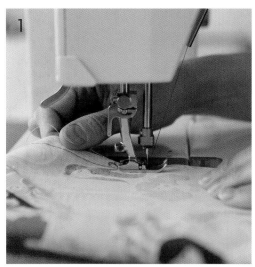

1 Cut thirteen 22 cm (8⅝ in) squares of turquoise patterned fabric and twelve squares of pink patterned cotton fabric. Arrange the squares in five rows of five squares, alternating the colours. With right sides facing and taking 1 cm (⅜ in) seam allowance, stitch each row together.

2 Press the seams of the first row in the same direction, the seams of the next row in the opposite direction and so on. With right sides facing and taking 1 cm (⅜ in) seam allowance, stitch the first and second row together, matching seams. Stitch the remaining rows to form a square. Press the seams downwards.

3 Lay a 112 cm (44 in) square of pink patterned fabric flat, wrong side up. This will be the backing fabric. Place the wadding on top. Centre the patchwork on top, smooth the layers outwards from the centre. Tack or pin together with curved basting pins. Tack the outer edges together.

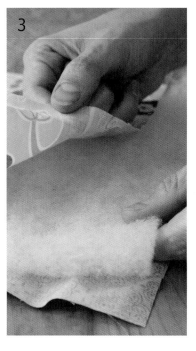

4 Cut the backing fabric and wadding 1 cm (⅜ in) larger all round than the patchwork. Cut two 104 x 9.5 cm (40⅞ x 3¾ in) and two 107 x 9.5 cm (42⅛ x 3¾ in) strips of pink fabric for the binding. Make the binding using a 5 cm (2 in) bias binding maker (see page 17).

5 Stitch the shorter bindings to the side edges of the play mat (see attaching bias bindings technique, page 18), taking a 2 cm (¾ in) seam allowance.

6 Fold and pin the binding over the edge of the play mat. Slipstitch the pressed edge of the bindings along the seams.

7 With 1.5 cm (⅝ in) extra at each end, stitch the remaining bindings to the raw edges. Fold and pin the binding over the edge of the play mat, turning in the ends to start and finish. Slipstitch the pressed edges along the seams.

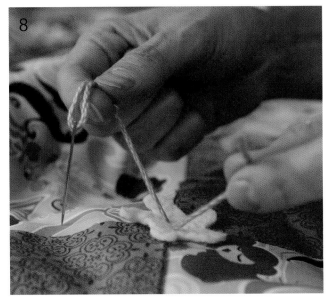

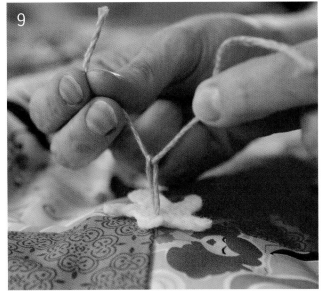

8 Use the template on page 122 to cut sixteen starfish shapes from yellow felt. Pin a starfish on each inner corner of the patchwork squares. Thread a large-eyed needle with a length of embroidery thread. Insert the needle through the centre of one starfish, through all the layers, leaving a trailing length of thread. Bring the needle to the right side close to where it emerged.

9 Tie the embroidery threads tightly together with a double knot. Trim the thread ends 1.5 cm (⅝ in) above the knot. Repeat on each starfish. Remove the tacking or basting pins.

TIP Remember to buy a larger amount of fabric if you wish to centre motifs on the patchwork squares (see positioning motifs technique, page 14).

potpourri sachet

Freshen your wardrobe with an elegant sachet of fragrant lavender. Make the sachet from a fine, loosely woven fabric to allow the scent to escape. As a finishing touch, trim the sachet with a velvet ribbon and button.

you will need

- 20 cm (¼ yd) of 90 cm (36 in) wide loosely woven lightweight cotton or linen pale turquoise fabric

- matching sewing threads

- pale turquoise stranded cotton embroidery thread

- crewel embroidery needle

- 2 handfuls of dried lavender

- 30 cm (⅓ yd) of 6 mm (¼ in) wide green velvet ribbon

- 2 cm (¾ in) diameter pale turquoise button

1 Cut two 15 cm (6 in) squares of loosely woven lightweight cotton or linen pale turquoise fabric. With right sides facing and taking 1 cm (⅜ in) seam allowance, stitch the outer edges leaving a 6.5 cm (2⅝ in) opening centrally along one edge to turn right side out.

2 Trim the seam allowance to 6 mm (¼ in) and snip the corners. Turn the square right side out and press.

3 Using four strands of cotton embroidery thread, sew a 2.5 cm (1 in) deep border on the square with a running stitch, leaving a gap to match the gap on the outer edge. Do not remove the needle and thread.

4 Fill the inner square with dried lavender. Finish the running stitch to close the gap and enclose the lavender. Slipstitch the gap on the outer edge closed.

5 Bend the ribbon into a loop. Overlap the ribbon 4.5 cm (1¾ in) from the ends. Sew securely to the top corner of the inner square as a hanging loop. Sew a button on top. Cut the ends of the ribbon diagonally to prevent fraying.

clothes envelope

Make a fabric envelope to store delicate clothing. The envelope would make a delightful gift especially when it is enhanced with a pretty flower brooch. The flower petals are made using a rouleau and have a button centre. The brooch is pinned to the flap of the envelope and can be removed to wear.

you will need

- 50 cm (½ yd) of 112 cm (44 in) wide pink plain cotton fabric

- 30 cm (⅓ yd) of 112 cm (44 in) wide pale green patterned cotton fabric

- matching sewing threads

- 40 cm (½ yd) of 90 cm (36 in) wide medium sew-on interfacing

- 1.8 cm (¾ in) press stud

- 30 cm (⅓ yd) of 112 cm (44 in) wide pale green plain cotton fabric

- 2 cm (¾ in) diameter pale green plain button

- 2 cm (¾ in) brooch pin

1 Cut one 63 x 13 cm (24¾ x 5¼ in) rectangle of plain pink fabric, two of pale green patterned fabric and three of interfacing. Tack the interfacing to the wrong side of the fabric pieces.

2 With right sides facing, pin and stitch the plain fabric between the patterned fabric rectangles along the long edges, taking 1.5 cm (⅝ in) seam allowance. Trim the interfacing in the seam allowance. Press the seams open.

3 Cut one 63 x 33 cm (24¾ x 13¼ in) rectangle of plain pink fabric for the lining. With right sides facing, pin and stitch the lining to the envelope taking 1.5 cm (⅝ in) seam allowance, leaving a gap to turn along one short edge. Trim the seam allowance to layer the seam. Snip the corners and turn right side out.

4 Press the lining to the inside. Slipstitch the opening closed. With the right side outside, press over 15 cm (6 in) at one end of the envelope for the flap. Open the flap out flat. Press over 20 cm (8 in) at the other end to form the envelope. Tack close to the side edges. Topstitch close to the side edges then 7.5 mm (⁵⁄₁₆ in) inside the side edges.

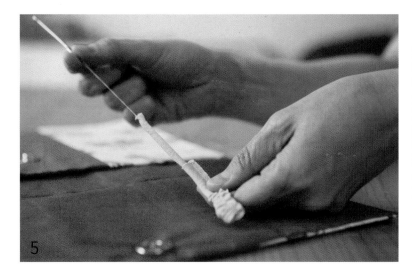

5 Sew a press-stud under the flap. Sew the corresponding press-stud to the front of the envelope, slip some clothing into the envelope to help judge the positioning. Cut a 30 x 2.5 cm (11⅞ x 1 in) bias strip of pale green plain fabric. Fold lengthwise in half with right sides facing. Stitch the long edges taking 6 mm (¼ in) seam allowance. Turn right side out with a bodkin to make a rouleau.

6 The rouleau will have stretched so trim the ends so it is 30 cm (12 in) long. Divide the rouleau into five 6 cm (2⅜ in) sections, mark each division with a pin. Anchor a double length of thread to one end. Fold each section into a loop for a petal, matching the pins to the ends of the rouleau at the centre of the 'flower'. Stitch through the folds and remove the pins.

7 Join the ends securely at the centre. Sew a button to the centre of the flower. Sew a brooch pin to the back of the flower. Pin the flower to the flap of the envelope.

tissue case

This beautiful case is made for a standard sized box of tissues. It's quick to make and is an ideal get-well-soon gift for a special friend. It would look equally good in a bathroom or guest bedroom. A row of co-ordinating buttons is a neat finishing detail.

you will need

- 35 cm (14 in) square of plain turquoise fabric
- 30 cm (⅓ yd) of 112 cm (44 in) wide patterned turquoise and green fabric
- matching sewing threads
- 3 x 1.2 cm (½ in) green buttons

1 Cut two 29 x 6 cm (11⅜ x 2⅜ in) bias strips of plain fabric. Press the strips lengthwise in half with wrong sides facing to make a double bias binding. Cut a 32 x 29 cm (12⅝ x 11⅜ in) rectangle of patterned fabric. Using a zigzag stitch, stitch the long raw edges to neaten them.

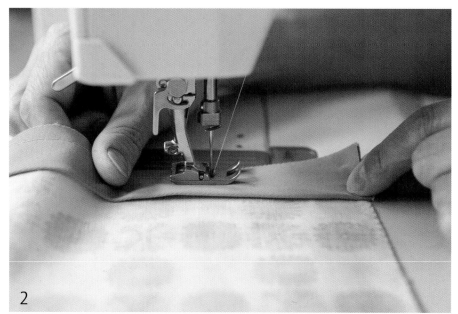

2 Taking a 7.5 mm (⁵⁄₁₆ in) seam allowance, stitch one binding to the wrong side of one short edge of the rectangle. Repeat on the other short edge.

3 Press the seams towards the binding. Fold the binding over the seam allowance and pin the pressed edge along the stitching on the right side. Topstitch close to the inner pressed edges.

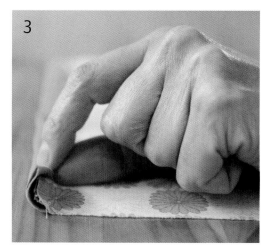

4 With right sides facing, fold the bound edges to meet at the centre of the long edges. Stitch the raw edges, taking 1.5 cm (⅝ in) seam allowance, stitch back and forth a few times over the ends of the binding to reinforce the seam.

5 Open the case and lay one seam out flat at one corner. Fold one end of the seam allowance to form a triangle. Stitch across the raw edge of the triangle to form a dart. Repeat at each corner.

6 Turn the tissue case right side out. Slip a pile of tissues inside. Sew three buttons in a row along the seam of one binding.

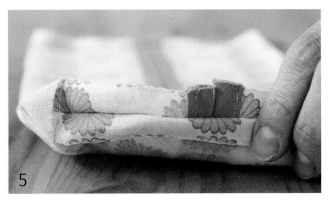

drawstring bag

Ribbon weaving is a great way to use up offcuts of ribbon and add interest and texture to this otherwise traditional drawstring bag. Choose ribbons to match the fabric of the bag then add a contrast colour too such as the turquoise on this pink and cream bag.

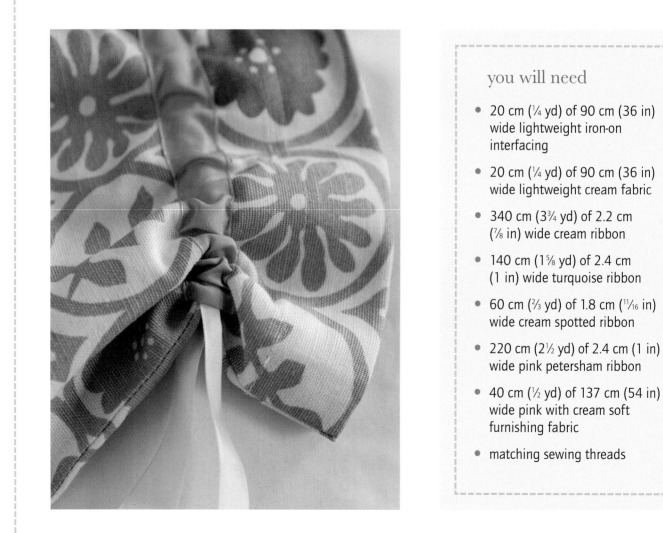

you will need

- 20 cm (¼ yd) of 90 cm (36 in) wide lightweight iron-on interfacing

- 20 cm (¼ yd) of 90 cm (36 in) wide lightweight cream fabric

- 340 cm (3¾ yd) of 2.2 cm (⅞ in) wide cream ribbon

- 140 cm (1⅝ yd) of 2.4 cm (1 in) wide turquoise ribbon

- 60 cm (⅔ yd) of 1.8 cm (¹¹⁄₁₆ in) wide cream spotted ribbon

- 220 cm (2½ yd) of 2.4 cm (1 in) wide pink petersham ribbon

- 40 cm (½ yd) of 137 cm (54 in) wide pink with cream soft furnishing fabric

- matching sewing threads

1 Cut one 36.5 x 17.5 cm (14⅜ x 6⅞ in) rectangle of lightweight iron-on interfacing and lightweight cream cotton fabric. Lay the interfacing glue side up on the ironing board. Draw a 1.5 cm (⅝ in) seam allowance within the outer edges with a water-erasable pen. For the warp (vertical) ribbons, cut eight 17.5 cm (6⅞ in) lengths of cream ribbon, four 17.5 cm (6⅞ in) lengths of turquoise ribbon and three 17.5 cm (6⅞ in) lengths of cream spotted ribbon.

2 Place one cream ribbon 1.5 cm (⅝ in) in from one short edge. Pin at the upper edge. Next, pin a turquoise ribbon, a cream ribbon then a cream spotted ribbon. Repeat this sequence twice then pin a cream ribbon, a turquoise ribbon and a cream ribbon.

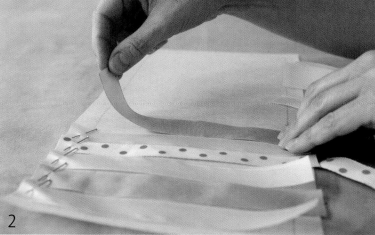

3 Cut six 36.5 cm (14⅜ in) lengths of pink petersham ribbon for the weft (horizontal) ribbons. Weave the weft ribbons in and out of the pinned ribbons. Pin the ribbons at the ends, keep the woven area within the drawn seam allowance.

4 With a moderate dry iron, press the ends of the ribbons to fuse them to the interfacing. Press the entire surface of the weaving, gradually removing the pins as you iron. Turn the weaving over and iron the wrong side. Tack the weaving right side up on the lightweight cream fabric rectangle.

5 Cut two 38 x 36.5 cm (15 x 14⅜ in) rectangles of pink soft furnishing fabric for the bag. With right sides facing, pin and stitch the weaving between one short edge of each bag taking 1.5 cm (⅝ in) seam allowance. Neaten the seams with a zigzag stitch. Press the seams towards the bags. Topstitch the bags close to the seams.

6 Cut two 33 cm (13 in) lengths of turquoise ribbon for the channels. Press under 6 mm (¼ in) twice on each end. Hand stitch the ends in place. With right sides facing up, pin the channels centrally 11.5 cm (4½ in) below the upper short edges of the bags. Stitch close to both long edges of the channels.

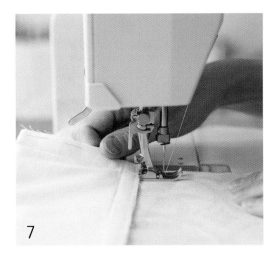

7 Fold the bag in half with right sides facing and matching the weaving seams. Pin and stitch the side edges taking 1.5 cm (⅝ in) seam allowance. Snip the corners then press the seams open. Neaten the seams with a zigzag stitch.

8 Press under 1 cm (⅜ in) then press 4 cm (1½ in) to the inside at the upper edge. Stitch close to the inner pressed edge to hem the bag. Cut the remaining cream ribbon in half. Using a bodkin, thread one length through the channels. Knot the ends together. Trim the ribbon ends diagonally. Repeat with other ribbon, starting at the other end of the channels.

shopping bag

This small chic and practical shopping bag has useful pockets on the sides for extra storage. It has ready-made handles which are available from haberdashery shops and departments. They give a highly professional finish to hand-made bags. The bag measures 40 x 30 cm (15¾ x 12 in), excluding the handles.

you will need

- 40 cm (½ yd) of 112 cm (44 in) wide green patterned cotton fabric

- 80 cm (1 yd) of 112 cm (44 in) wide green dotted cotton fabric

- matching sewing threads

- 80 cm (1 yd) of 90 cm (36 in) wide medium sew-in interfacing

- 2 x 16.5 cm (6½ in) D-shaped amber plastic bag handles

1 Use the template on page 123 to cut two shopping bags to the fold from both fabrics and interfacing. Cut two 20.5 x 19 cm (8 x 7½ in) rectangles of green patterned fabric and interfacing for the pockets. Tack the interfacing to the wrong side of the green patterned fabric pieces.

2 Press under 1 cm (⅜ in) then 1.5 cm (⅝ in) on the upper short edges of the pockets. Stitch close to both edges to hem the pockets. Press under 1.5 cm (⅝ in) on the raw edges of the pockets.

3 With right sides facing up, pin each pocket centrally to a bag with the short lower edge 4.5 cm (1¾ in) above the lower edge of the bags. Topstitch close to the side and lower edges of the pockets. Stitch again 6 mm (¼ in) inside the first stitching. Cut four 37 x 14 cm (14½ x 5½ in) rectangles of green dotted fabric and two of interfacing for the bands.

4 Tack the interfacing to the wrong side of two bands. With right sides facing, pin and stitch the bands between the bags along the long straight edges taking 1.5 cm (⅝ in) seam allowance. Trim the interfacing in the seam allowances and press the seams toward the bands. Topstitch the bands close to the seams.

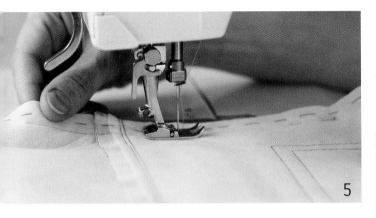

5

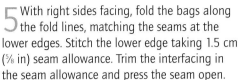

5 With right sides facing, fold the bags along the fold lines, matching the seams at the lower edges. Stitch the lower edge taking 1.5 cm (⅝ in) seam allowance. Trim the interfacing in the seam allowance and press the seam open.

6 Follow steps 4–5 to make the lining from the green dotted fabric pieces, omitting the interfacing and topstitching. Turn the lining right side out. Slip the lining in the bag with right sides facing, matching the raw edges. Pin and stitch the curved edges together taking 6 mm (¼ in) seam allowance. Clip the curves.

6

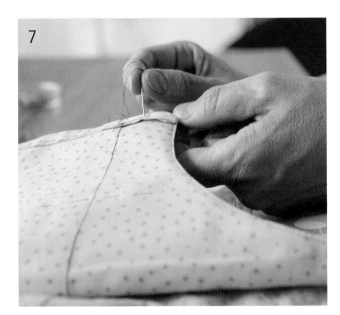

7

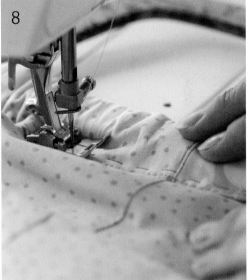

8

7 Turn the bag right side out by pulling the lining through the short upper edges. Press the lining inside the bag. Tack the lining and bag together 9 cm (3½ in) below the upper raw edges. Topstitch the bag close to the curved edges. Press and tack under 1 cm (⅜ in) on the upper raw edges.

8 Slip one upper edge through one bag handle. Pin the pressed edge to match the inner tacked line, forming a channel enclosing the handle. Tack, then stitch close to the pressed edge, laying the channel flat a section at a time to stitch in place. Stitch again 7.5 mm (⁵⁄₁₆ in) inside the pressed edge. Repeat to attach a bag handle to the other upper edge of the bag.

scallop cot quilt

This vibrant reversible quilt measures 100 x 75 cm (40 x 30 in), it would make a super cosy gift for a little one. Choose a striped fabric that has stripes running parallel with the selvedges, this will help you to keep the quilting lines straight as you simply follow the line of the stripes.

you will need

- thin card
- pen and ruler
- pattern paper or brown parcel paper
- 110 cm (1¼ yd) of 112 cm (44 in) wide cotton pink striped fabric
- 110 cm (1¼ yd) of 112 cm (44 in) wide cotton blue checkered fabric
- 110 cm (1¼ yd) of 90 cm (36 in) wide 56 g (2 oz) wadding
- matching sewing threads
- curved basting pins (optional)
- matching quilting thread

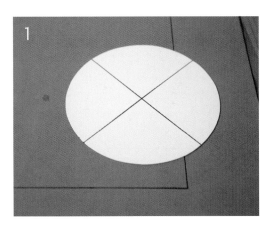

1 Cut a 12.5 cm (5 in) diameter circle of thin card to use as a template for drawing the scallops. Divide the circle into quarters with a pen and ruler. To make a pattern, cut a 100 x 75 cm (40 x 30 in) rectangle of pattern paper or brown parcel paper. Draw a 6.25 cm (2½ in) deep margin inside the rectangle.

2 Place the circle template on one corner, matching the quarter lines to the inner corner of the margin. Draw around three-quarters of the circle on the margin. Repeat on each corner. Move the template along the inner edges of the margin and draw a row of semi-circles edge to edge for the scallops. Cut out the pattern along the scalloped edges.

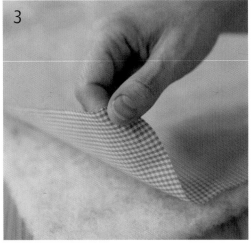

3 Cut a 104 x 79 cm (41½ x 31½ in) rectangle from both fabrics and wadding. Lay the striped fabric out flat wrong side up, pin the pattern centrally on top. Draw around the scallops with an air-erasable fabric pen. Lay the checkered fabric right side up on the wadding. Smooth the fabric outwards from the centre.

4 With right sides facing, place the striped fabric on top of the checkered fabric and wadding. Working outwards from the centre, smooth the fabric outwards and tack or pin the layers together using curved basting pins.

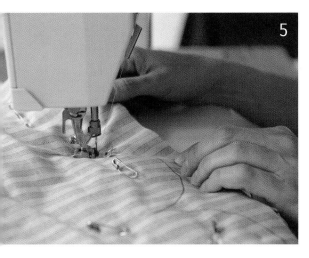

5 Starting on the curve of one scallop, stitch along the drawn lines, leaving a 37.5 cm (15 in) gap on one edge to turn right side out. Remove the tacking or basting pins.

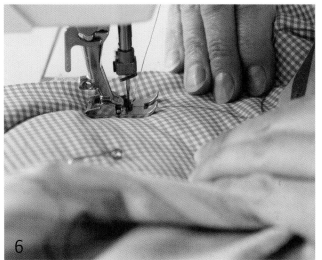

6 On the right side of the checkered fabric, use the pattern to draw the unstitched scallops with an air-erasable fabric pen. Tack or re-pin the edges of the gap. Stitch along the drawn lines to secure the wadding to the checkered fabric. Do not catch in the striped fabric. Continue stitching the scallops on the striped fabric but without stitching through the checkered fabric and wadding.

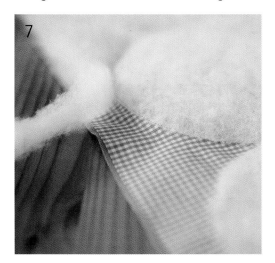

7 Trim away the wadding in the seam allowance close to the stitching. Trim the seam allowance to 6 mm (¼ in). Carefully snip the curves and corners. Turn right side out and gently press the edges of the scallops. Turn the raw edges of the gap to the inside along the stitching and slipstitch the scallops together.

8 Tack the layers together or pin with curved basting pins. Lay the quilt out flat, striped side up. Thread the sewing machine with quilting thread. Starting at the centre at the top of the quilt, stitch between the inner corners of the scallops, following the lines of the stripes with the sewing machine set to a long stitch length.

picnic rug

There is always plenty to take on a picnic. This cosy picnic rug makes life easy as it can be folded in half, rolled up and fastened with straps and D-rings. A handy wrist band keeps your hands free to carry that all-important hamper. The rug measures 130 cm (51 in) square.

you will need

- 130 cm (51 in) square of green fleece

- 30 cm (12 in) diameter circle of paper or a plate

- 1 m (1¼ yd) of 112 cm (44 in) wide green patterned fabric

- 20 cm (¼ yd) of 90 cm (36 in) wide light sew-in interfacing

- 4 x 2.5 cm (1 in) D-rings

- 5 cm (2 in) bias binding maker

1 To shape the rug, round off the corners of the
fleece by placing a 30 cm (12 in) diameter
plate or circle on one corner. Draw around the
circle between the adjacent side edges of the rug
with an air-erasable pen. Cut along the curve.
Repeat on the other corners.

2 From patterned fabric and interfacing, cut
two 43 x 7.5 cm (17 x 2⅞ in) straight strips
for the straps and one 40 x 7.5 cm (15¾ x 2⅞ in)
straight strip for the wrist band. Tack the
interfacing to the wrong side of the fabric pieces.
Press lengthwise in half with the wrong sides
facing. Open out flat then press under 1 cm
(⅜ in) on the long edges.

3 Press under 1 cm (⅜ in) on one end of each
strap. Refold in half. Topstitch close to the
pressed edges of the straps and wrist band. Pin
and tack the raw end of one strap to the rug on
one edge close to a curved corner. Tack the
other strap to the rug 31.5 cm (12⅜ in) from the
first strap on the same edge of the rug. Fold the
wrist band in half. Tack the raw ends to the rug
next to the second strap.

4 Cut two 7.5 cm (2⅞ in) squares of patterned fabric and
interfacing for the D-ring holders, tack the interfacing to
the wrong side. Fold in half with right sides facing. Stitch the
long edges, taking 1 cm (⅜ in) seam allowances. Trim the seam
allowances, turn right side out and press.

5 Slip two D-rings onto each D-ring holder. Pin the raw ends together and tack on top of the straps, matching the raw ends.

6 From patterned fabric, cut 9.5 cm (3¾ in) wide bias strips measuring a total of 5 m (5½ yds) for the binding. Join the strips and make a continuous length of bias binding using a 5 cm (2 in) bias binding maker (see page 17).

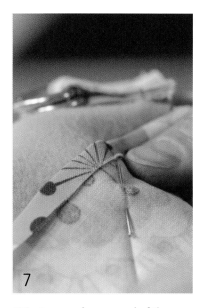

7 Press under one end of the binding to start. Refer to the Attaching Bias Binding technique on page 18 to bind the rug, taking 2 cm (¾ in) seam allowance. Ease the binding around the corners. Cut off the excess binding 1.5 cm (⅝ in) beyond the start of the binding.

8 Fold the binding over the edge of the blanket, and tack the pressed edge along the seam. Topstitch the binding close to the pressed edge.

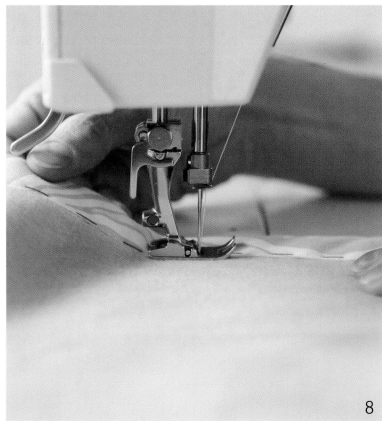

beach bag

Pack all you need for a fun day at the beach into this deep and roomy beach bag. Choose two contrasting fabrics that work well together, the bag has a distinctive band and shoulder strap that matches the lining. The bag measures 32 cm (12½ in) wide x 40 cm (15¾ in) high.

you will need

- 50 cm (⅝ yd) of 137 cm (54 in) wide green spotted soft furnishing fabric

- 70 cm (¾ yd) of 90 cm (36 in) wide medium sew-in interfacing

- 80 cm (⅞ yd) of 112 cm (44 in) wide pink patterned cotton fabric

- matching sewing threads

- 30 cm (⅓ yd) of 90 cm (36 in) wide light sew-in interfacing

- 2 x 5 cm (2 in) D-rings

1 Refer to the diagram on page 124 to cut two bags from green spotted fabric and medium sew-in interfacing. Cut two 43 x 8 cm (16¾ x 3¼ in) bands of pink patterned fabric and medium sew-in interfacing. Tack the interfacing to the wrong side of the fabric pieces.

2 With right sides facing, pin and stitch the bands to the upper edges of the bag, taking 1.5 cm (⅝ in) seam allowance. Press the seams open. With right sides facing, pin and stitch the side edges of the bags, matching the band seams, taking 1.5 cm (⅝ in) seam allowance. Press the seams open.

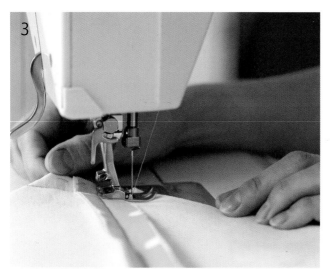

3 With right sides facing, pin and stitch the base of the bag, taking 1.5 cm (⅝ in) seam allowance. Press the seam open. With right sides facing, fold the lower ends of the side seams to match the ends of the base seam. Stitch the raw edges, taking 1.5 cm (⅝ in) seam allowance.

4 From pink patterned fabric and light sew-in interfacing, cut two 13 x 7 cm (5¼ x 2¾ in) rectangles for the D-ring holders and one 77 x 13 cm (30¼ x 5¼ in) strip for the strap. Tack the interfacing to the wrong side of the fabric pieces. With right sides facing, fold the D-rings in half, stitch the short edges, taking a 1.5 cm (⅝ in) seam allowance.

5 Turn right side out and press in half. Slip a ring onto each D-ring holder. Turn the bag right side out. Pin the raw ends of the D-ring holders together and stitch to the upper edge of the bands over the seams, taking a 1 cm (⅜ in) seam allowance.

6 With right sides facing, fold the strap lengthwise in half, stitch the long edges, taking 1.5 cm (⅝ in) seam allowance. Turn right side out and press. Turn 1 cm (⅜ in) at each end to the inside. Tack in place. Slip the strap through the D-rings. Tack the pressed ends 2.5 cm (1 in) above the D-rings. Stitch close to the pressed ends then 6 mm (¼ in) from the first stitching.

7 Refer to the diagram on page 124 to cut two linings from pink patterned fabric. With right sides facing and taking 1.5 cm (⅝ in) seam allowance, stitch the side seams, leaving a gap in one seam to turn right side out. Press the seams open. Follow step 3 to stitch the base. With right sides facing, insert the bag in the lining, matching the seams. Pin and stitch the upper edge, taking a 1.5 cm (⅝ in) seam allowance.

8 Turn right side out. Slipstitch the gap closed. Press the lining to the inside. Topstitch close to the upper edge then 6 mm (¼ in) below. Fold and pin the bag 4 cm (1½ in) from the side and base seams. Topstitch 4 mm (⁵⁄₃₂ in) from the folds, finishing 4 mm (⁵⁄₃₂ in) from short seams at the ends of the base seams.

wall tidy

Encourage a well-organized workspace with this vibrant wall tidy. The pockets are pleated to provide storage for stationery or small toys. Stiffening the pockets with interfacing keeps the pleats sharp. The wall tidy measures 59 x 38 cm (23 x 15 in), metal eyelets are fixed to the top so it can be hung on hooks.

you will need

- 20 cm (¼ yd) each of 112 cm (44 in) wide green patterned fabric, blue patterned fabric and pink striped fabric

- matching sewing threads

- 120 cm (1⅓ yd) of (90 cm) wide firm iron-on interfacing

- 80 cm (1 yd) of 137 cm (54 in) wide yellow spotted fabric

- 18 mm (¾ in) wide bias binding maker

- 2 x 32 cm (12⅝ in) lengths of 18 x 4 mm (¾ x ⁵⁄₃₂ in) half round stripwood

- 2 x 1.5 cm (⅝ in) metal eyelets and fixing kit

- pin hammer

1 Cut one 58 x 18.5 cm (23¼ x 7¼ in) strip of green and one of blue patterned fabric and two of interfacing for the pockets. Fuse the interfacing to the wrong side of the pockets. Press under 1 cm (⅜ in) then 1.5 cm (⅝ in) on the long upper edge. Stitch close to both pressed edges to hem the pockets.

2 With the pockets right side up, refer to the diagram on page 124 to make the pleats by bringing the solid lines to the broken lines. Press the pleats and tack across the lower edges. Cut one 72 x 38 cm (28¼ x 15 in) rectangle of yellow spotted fabric and interfacing for the wall tidy. Fuse the interfacing to the wrong side of the wall tidy. Neaten the short upper and lower edges of the wall tidy with a zigzag stitch.

3 Pin the pockets to the wall tidy, with the upper edge of the green pocket 22 cm (8⅝ in) below the upper edge of the wall tidy and the lower raw edge of the blue pocket 11.5 cm (4⅝ in) above the lower edge of the wall tidy. Tack the side and lower edges of the pockets. To form the separate pockets, stitch between the centre pleats.

4 Cut one 38 x 3.5 cm (15 x 1⅜ in) straight strip of green and one of blue patterned fabric. Make a binding using an 18 mm (¾ in) bias binding maker (see making bias binding technique, page 17). Pin and tack the binding over the lower edge of the pockets, matching the lower edge of the pockets to the centre of the binding. Stitch close to both long edges of the binding.

5 Press under 8.5 cm (3⅜ in) on the upper edge and 4.5 cm (1⅞ in) on the lower edge of the wall tidy. On the right side, topstitch close to the pressed edges. Stitch 4 cm (1½ in) then 3 cm (1¼ in) below the upper edge. Stitch 3 cm (1¼ in) above the lower edge. Insert a 32 cm (12⅝ in) length of 18 x 4 mm (¾ x 5/32 in) stripwood through the 3 cm (1¼ in) wide channels. Tack across the ends of the channels.

6 Cut two 62 x 8 cm (24¼ x 3 in) straight strips of pink striped fabric for the side bindings. Press the bindings lengthwise in half with wrong sides facing. Open out flat and press the long edges to meet at the centre. Press under 1.5 cm (⅝ in) at each end of the bindings.

7 Slip one long edge of the wall tidy inside one binding. Tack through all the layers. Slipstitch the ends together enclosing the upper and lower edges of the wall tidy. Repeat on the other long edge of the wall tidy. Stitch close to the inner pressed edges of the bindings.

8 Fix a metal eyelet 2.5 cm (1 in) inside each side edge at the top of the wall tidy using a pin hammer and following the manufacturer's instructions.

buttoned blind

Choose two pretty fabrics that work well together to make this neat button-up blind. A pair of loops at the bottom of the blind can fasten onto buttons along the side edges to raise the blind to different levels. The fabric quantities needed will depend upon the size of the blind.

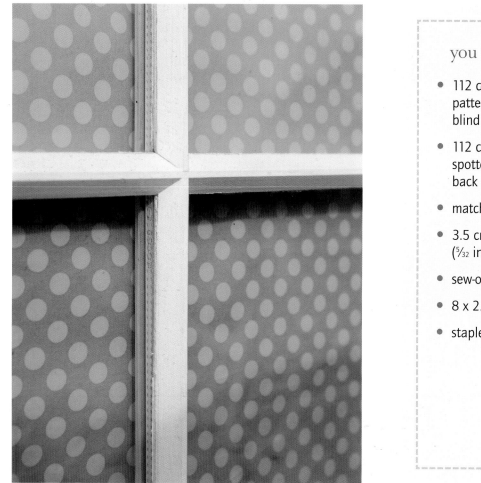

you will need

- 112 cm (44 in) wide turquoise patterned cotton fabric for blind front

- 112 cm (44 in) wide green spotted cotton fabric for blind back

- matching sewing threads

- 3.5 cm (1⅜ in) wide x 4 mm (⁵⁄₃₂ in) thick strip wood batten

- sew-on touch-and-close tape

- 8 x 2.3 cm (⅞ in) buttons

- staple gun

1 Measure the intended width and drop of the blind. Cut a square or rectangle of both fabrics with 1.5 cm (⅝ in) added to all edges for seam allowances. Cut a 15 x 2.5 cm (6 x 1 in) wide bias strip of the blind back fabric for the button loops. Fold the strip lengthwise in half with right sides facing. Stitch the long edges taking 6 mm (¼ in) seam allowance.

2 Turn right side out with a bodkin and cut in half to make two button loops. Tack each button loop to the lower edge of the blind front on the right side, 2.5 cm (1 in) in from the side edges with a 2 cm (¾ in) gap within each loop.

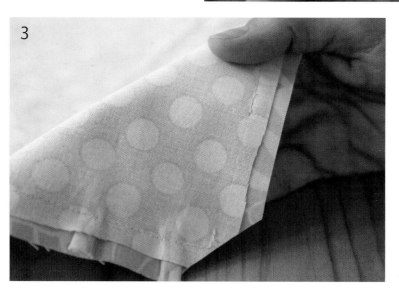

3 Pin the front and back blinds together with right sides facing. Taking a 1.5 cm (⅝ in) seam allowance, stitch the side and lower edges, leaving a 4.5 cm (1¾ in) gap 2 cm (¾ in) above the lower edge in one side seam. Trim the seam allowances to layer them and clip the corners.

4 Turn the blind right side out and press it. Press under 1.5 cm (⅝ in) on the upper edge. Cut touch-and-close tape 6 mm (¼ in) shorter than the width of the blind. Pull the tapes apart. Pin one tape to the upper edge of the blind 3 mm (⅛ in) inside the upper and side edges. Stitch close to the edges of the tape.

5 Topstitch close to the lower edge then 5 cm (2 in) above the lower edge to form a channel. Saw two pieces of strip wood 6 mm (¼ in) shorter than the width of the blind. Insert one batten through the channel. Slipstitch the gap closed.

6 Divide the side edges into fifths and mark the divisions on each side edge with a pin. Sew a button at each division 3 cm (1¼ in) in from the side edges. Screw the remaining wood batten above the window. Use a staple gun to staple the corresponding touch-and-close tape to the batten. Press the upper edge of the blind to the batten to fix in place.

lampshade

Transform a ready-made drum lampshade into a stylish new version trimmed with a border of flamboyant rouleau coils. If you are feeling adventurous, cover the entire lampshade with coils for a lavish effect.

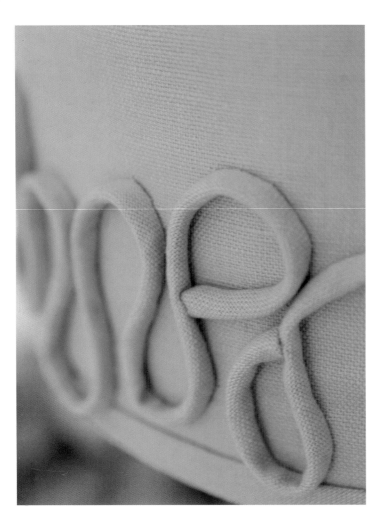

you will need

- drum lampshade approximately 20 cm (8 in) tall x 25 cm (10 in) diameter

- Approximately 1 m (1¼ yd) of 90 cm (36 in) wide turquoise linen

- matching sewing threads

- 1.5 cm (½ in) bias binding maker

- fabric glue

- glue spreader

- rouleau turner (optional)

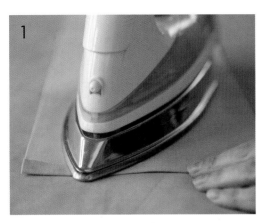

1 Measure the circumference and height of the lampshade. Cut a rectangle of linen to cover the lampshade that is the circumference measurement plus 3 cm (1¼ in) x 6 mm (¼ in) less than the height. Press under 1.2 cm (½ in) on one short edge of the cover.

2 Starting at the seam of the lampshade, wrap the cover around the lampshade 3 mm (⅛ in) below the upper edge. Smooth the cover around the lampshade and lap the pressed edge over the other end and pin in position. Slipstitch the pressed edge in place.

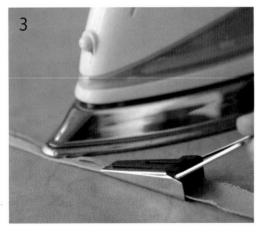

3 Cut two 2.5 cm (1 in) wide bias strips measuring the circumference of the lampshade plus 3 cm (1¼ in) in length for the bindings. Use the strips to make two lengths of bias binding using a 1.2 cm (½ in) bias binding maker (see making bias binding technique, page 17). Press under one end of the bindings.

4 Apply glue sparingly to the raw end of one binding with a glue spreader. Starting at the lampshade seam, start to glue the binding around the lower edge of the lampshade, covering the lower raw edge of the cover. Continue spreading glue and sticking the binding in place. Repeat on the upper edge of the lampshade, allowing the binding to extend 3 mm (⅛ in) above the lampshade.

5 Cut four 90 cm (36 in) lengths of 2.5 cm (1 in) wide bias strips for the rouleaux. Fold one strip lengthwise in half with right sides facing. Stitch the long edges taking 5 mm (³⁄₁₆ in) seam allowance.

6 Turn the rouleau right side out with a bodkin or rouleau turner. Repeat to make the other rouleaux. Poke in the raw ends of the rouleaux with the ends of a pair of embroidery scissors. Turn the lampshade upside down.

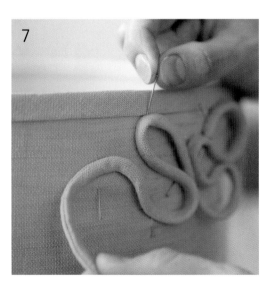

7 Measure and divide the lower edge of the lampshade into quarters and mark each division with a pin. Within one marked section, pin one rouleau in random curling shapes around the lower edge of the lampshade. Take care to pin through the fabric only and not the lampshade.

8 When you are happy with the design, catch the rouleaux to the fabric with small stitches. Remove the pins as you sew. Continue applying the rouleaux around the lampshade.

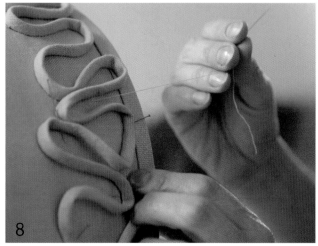

cupcake doorstop

Here is an amusing project that is practical too. This larger-than-life cupcake is weighted to hold a door open. It's fun to make and can be decorated with beads as lavishly or as simply as you wish. If you cannot find turquoise jumbo corduroy, dye white or cream jumbo corduroy to achieve the colour you want.

you will need

- 20 cm (¼ yd) of 90 cm (36 in) wide turquoise jumbo corduroy

- 40 cm (16 in) square of pink with orange spotted fabric

- matching sewing threads

- 9.5 cm (3¾ in) diameter circle of thin card

- 20 cm (8 in) square of pale yellow fleece

- 1 kg (2 lb) of rice

- Approximately 50 g (2 oz) polyester toy filling

- 2.5 cm (1 in) pink bead

- Approximately 7 x 4 mm (⁵⁄₃₂ in) pale orange beads

- Approximately 7 x 8 mm (⁵⁄₁₆ in) pink disc beads

2 Cut a 12 cm (4¾ in) diameter circle of corduroy for the base. Fold the base into quarters and mark each division at the circumference with a pin. Snip the seam allowance of the lower curved edge of the case. This will make it easier to stitch to the base. With right sides facing, pin the base to the snipped edge, matching the pins to the seams. Stitch, taking a 1 cm (⅜ in) seam allowance. Snip the curves.

1 Use the template on page 126 to cut four cases from corduroy, matching the arrow to the ridges of the corduroy. With right sides facing and taking a 1 cm (⅜ in) seam allowance, stitch the cases together along the short edges, forming a ring. Press the seams open.

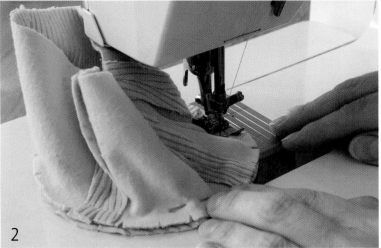

3 Use the template on page 125 to cut a cake from spotted fabric. Cut slits along the broken lines. With right sides facing, fold, matching the edges of the darts. Stitch the darts to the dots, taking 6 mm (¼ in) seam allowance. Snip the curves. Press the seams open.

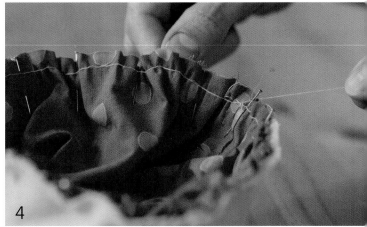

4 Gather the edge of the cake with a long stitch. With right sides facing, pin the cake and case together, matching seams to darts. Pull up the gathers and stitch, taking a 1 cm (⅜ in) seam allowance. Turn the doorstop right side out through the slits.

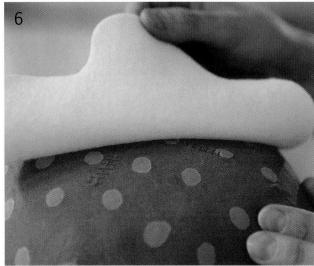

6 Use the template on page 126 to cut the icing from fleece. Pin the icing on the cake, making sure that it covers the sewn slits. Hand stitch in place with tiny stitches around the edges of the icing.

5 Position the card circle in the case on the base. Adjust the seam allowance to lie against the sides of the case. Pour the rice into the doorstop. Fill the rest of the doorstop with the toy filling. Ladder stitch the slits securely closed by bringing the edges of the slits together and working hand stitches over the joins.

7 Anchor a double length of sewing thread to the top of the icing. Thread on a 2.5 cm (1 in) pink bead and a 4 mm (5/32 in) pale orange bead. Insert the needle back through the first bead and pull the thread. Make a small stitch through the icing and repeat to secure. Sew the remaining beads at random to the icing.

TIP Corduroy has a nap which means the surface has a pile and appears different from different angles, so cut all the cases in the same direction.

Templates

Some of the projects in this book refer to templates and diagrams. Trace the templates onto tracing paper or enlarge on a photocopier where indicated. Remember to transfer any grain lines, fold lines and other useful information.

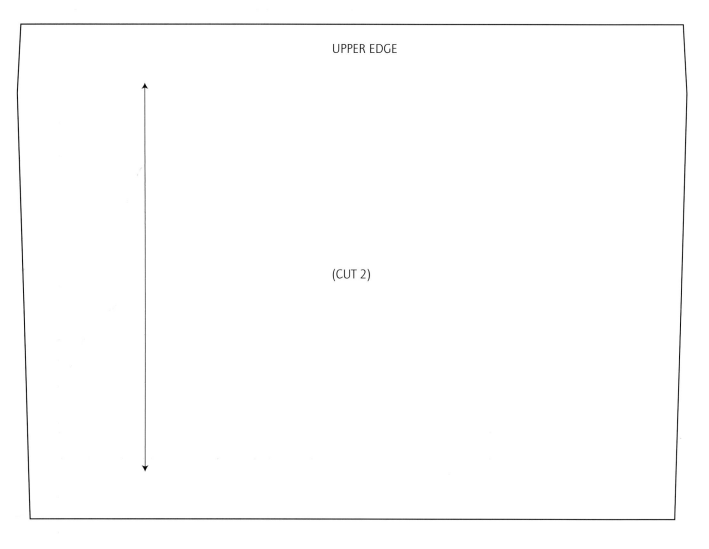

UPPER EDGE

(CUT 2)

stationery folder (pocket) (page 44)
Increase template size by 110%

pocketed napkin (pocket) (page 60)

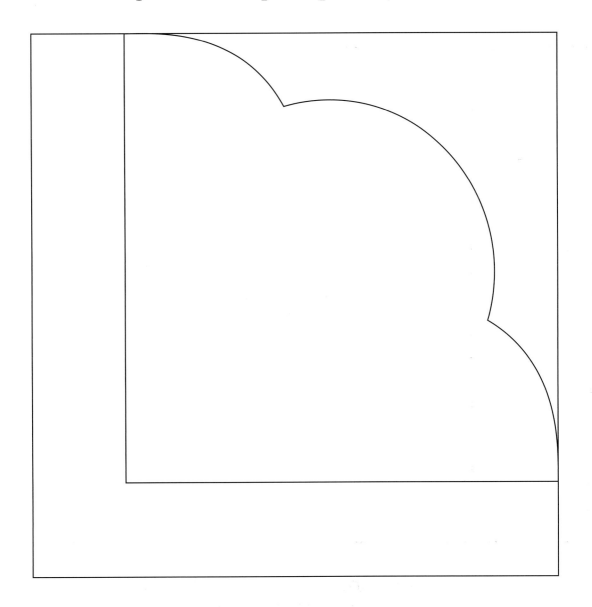

bordered throw (page 66)

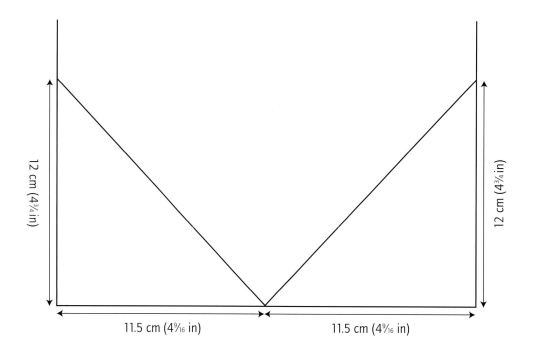

12 cm (4¾ in)

12 cm (4¾ in)

11.5 cm (4⁹⁄₁₆ in)

11.5 cm (4⁹⁄₁₆ in)

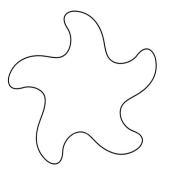

patchwork play mat (starfish) (page 68)

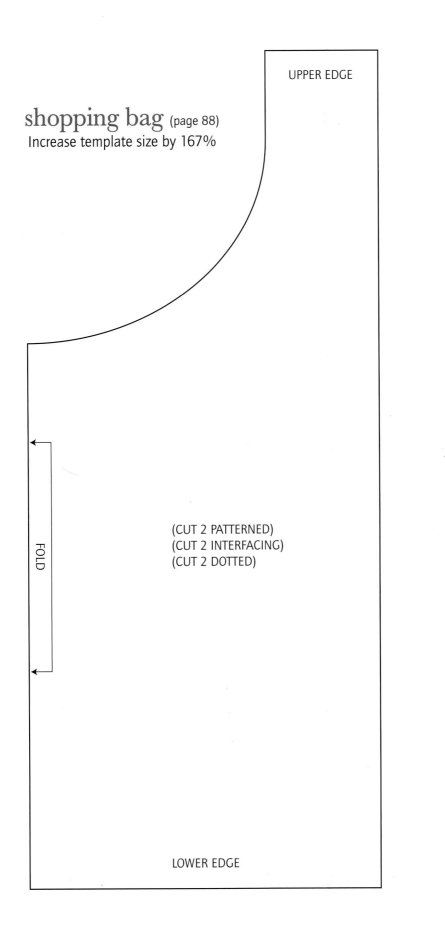

UPPER EDGE

shopping bag (page 88)
Increase template size by 167%

FOLD

(CUT 2 PATTERNED)
(CUT 2 INTERFACING)
(CUT 2 DOTTED)

LOWER EDGE

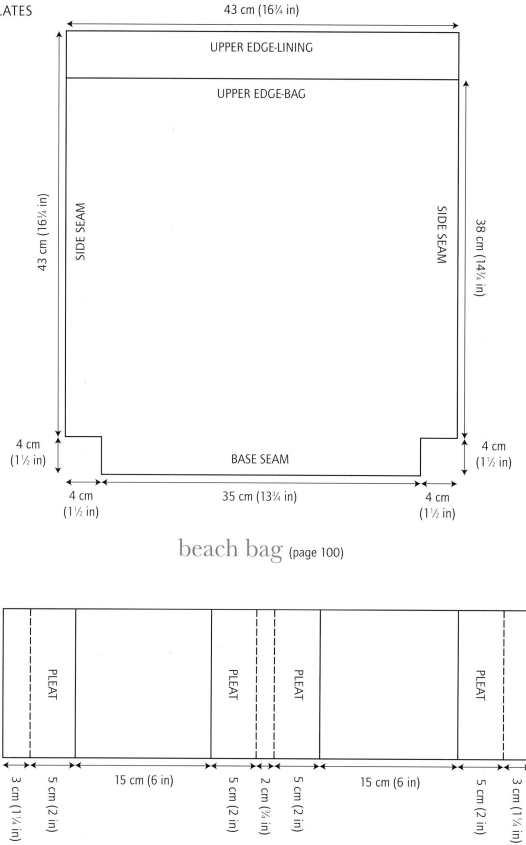

43 cm (16¾ in)

UPPER EDGE-LINING

UPPER EDGE-BAG

43 cm (16¾ in)

SIDE SEAM

SIDE SEAM

38 cm (14¾ in)

4 cm (1½ in)

BASE SEAM

4 cm (1½ in)

4 cm (1½ in)

35 cm (13¾ in)

4 cm (1½ in)

beach bag (page 100)

PLEAT

PLEAT

PLEAT

PLEAT

3 cm (1¼ in)

5 cm (2 in)

15 cm (6 in)

5 cm (2 in)

2 cm (¾ in)

5 cm (2 in)

15 cm (6 in)

5 cm (2 in)

3 cm (1¼ in)

wall tidy (pocket) (page 104)

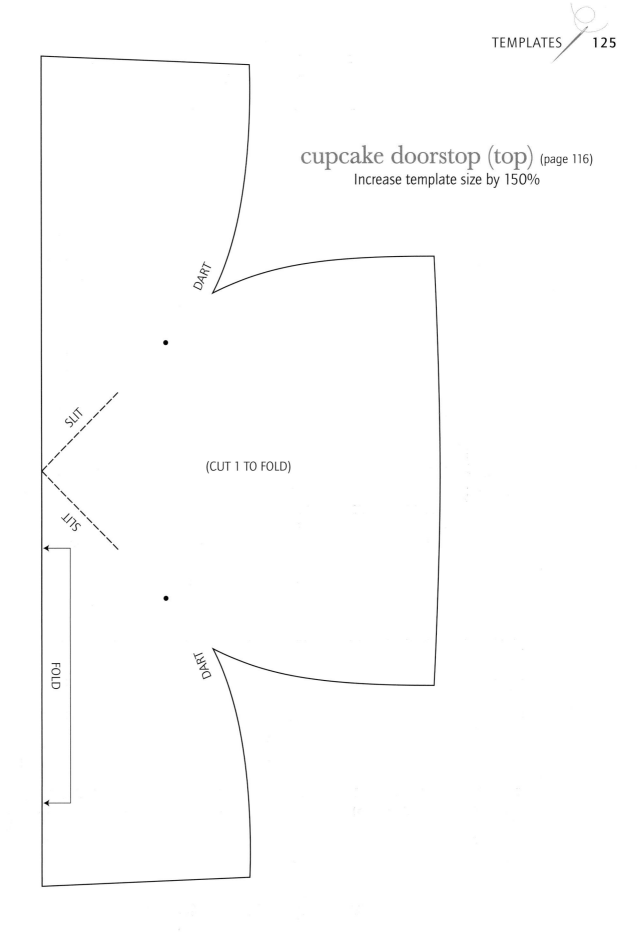

cupcake doorstop (top) (page 116)
Increase template size by 150%

DART

SLIT

SLIT

(CUT 1 TO FOLD)

FOLD

DART

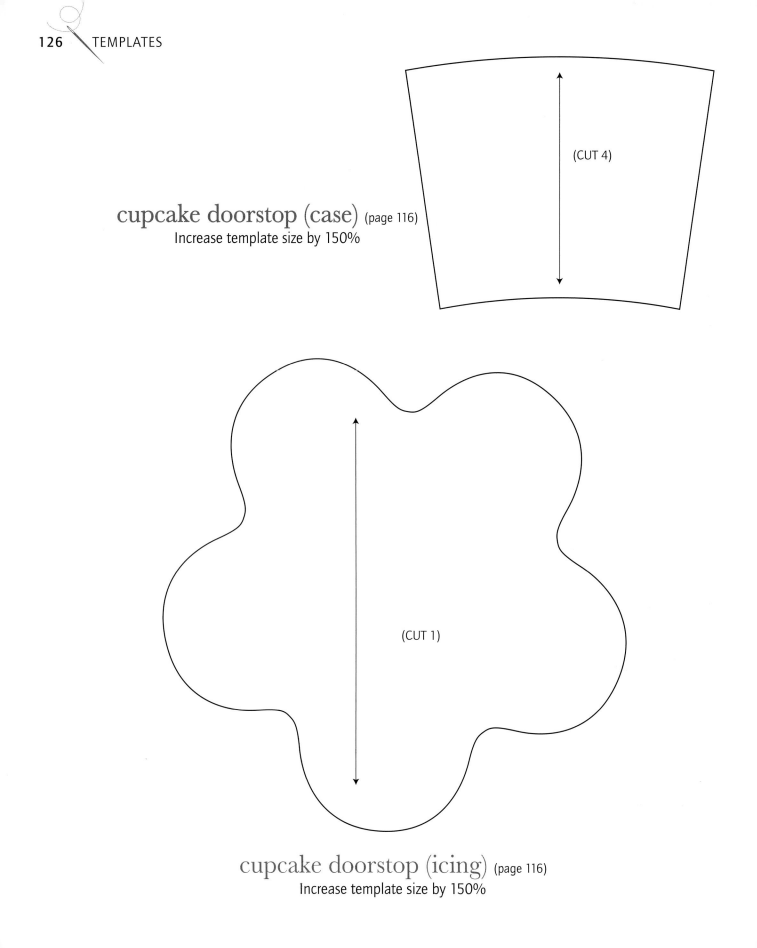

(CUT 4)

cupcake doorstop (case) (page 116)
Increase template size by 150%

(CUT 1)

cupcake doorstop (icing) (page 116)
Increase template size by 150%

Useful addresses

Bell House Fabrics
www.bellhousefabrics.co.uk
Tel: 01580 712555
(soft furnishing fabrics)

Dungarees and Daisies
www.dungareesanddaisies.co.uk
Tel: 01243 378872
(fabrics)

Fabric Inspirations
www.fabricinspirations.co.uk
Tel: 01158 418898
(fabrics)

Gone To Earth
www.gonetoearth.co.uk
Tel: 01933 623412
(fabrics)

21st Century Yarns
www.21stcenturyyarns.com
Tel: 07850 616537
(handmade felt)

Fun 2 Do
www.fun2do.co.uk
01228 523843
(bag handles)

Kleins
www.kleins.co.uk
Tel: 0207 437 6162
(haberdashery and trimmings)

MacCulloch and Wallis
www.macculloch-wallis.co.uk
Tel: 0207 629 0311
(haberdashery, trimmings and bag handles)

Index

bags
    Beach bag 100–103
    Drawstring bag 84–87
    handles 11
    Shopping bag 88–91
    Beach bag 100–103
bias binding 11
    maker 12
    making 17
    using bias strips 17
binding(s) 17, 18
bodkin 12
Bolster cushion 28–31
Bordered tablecloth 52–55
Bordered throw 66–67
Bound napkin 56–59
Box cushion 26–39
Buttoned blind 108–111
buttons 10

Clothes envelope 76–79
corners and curves, clipping
    16
cotton 10
Cupcake doorstop 116–119
cushions
    Bolster cushion 28–31
    Box cushion 26–39
    Cutwork cushion 24–27
    Pyramid cushion 32–35
    Tie-on cushion 40–43
cutting out 13
Cutwork cushion 24–27

Drawstring bag 84–87
D-rings 11

equipment 12

fabrics 10
    fabric-marking tools
    furnishing 10
fleece and felt 10

haberdashery 10–11

interfacing 10

Lampshade 112–15
linen 10

materials 10–11
mats
    Patchwork play mat 68–71
    Place mat 64–65
measuring tools 12
metal eyelets 11
motifs, positioning 14

napkins
    Bound napkin 56–59
    Pocketed napkin 60–63
needles 12

Patchwork play mat 68–71
pattern-making papers 12
pattern-making tools 12
Picnic rug 96–99
pins 12
piping 19–20
    attaching 21
    cord 11
    joining piping ends 20
    making 19
Place mat 64–65
Pocketed napkin 60–63
Potpourri sachet 72–75
press studs 11
Pyramid cushion 32–35

ribbons 10
Ripple table runner 48–51
rouleau turner 12
rouleaux 21

Scallop cot quilt 92–95
scissors 12
seams 15
    layering 15
    neatening 16
sewing workbox 13

Shopping bag 88–91
slipstitching 16
Stationery folder 44–47
stitching 15

tacking 15
tear-away stabilizer 10
techniques 13–21
templates and patterns,
using 14
threads 11
Tie-on cushion 40–43
Tissue case 80–83
touch-and-close tape 11
trimmings 11

wadding 10
Wall tidy 104–107

zippers 11